D1583064

But at my back I always hear
Time's winged chariot hurrying near;
And yonder all before us lie
Deserts of vast eternity.
ANDREW MARVELL

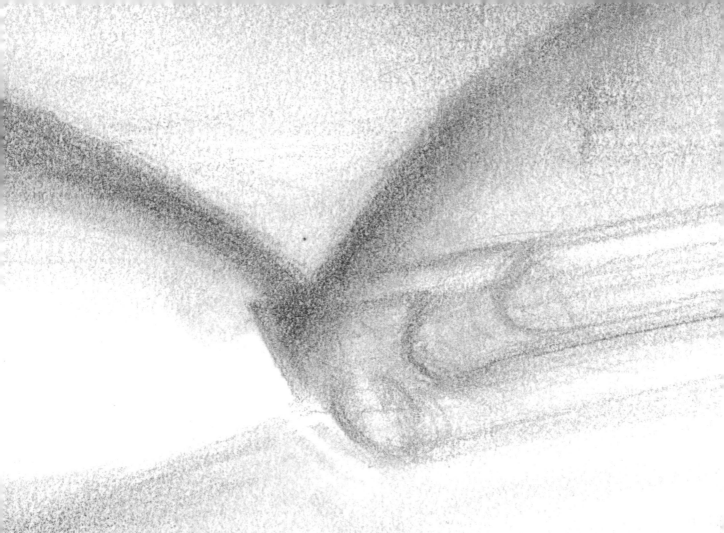

TIME FOR
LIGHTS OUT

Raymond Briggs

JONATHAN CAPE
LONDON

1 3 5 7 9 10 8 6 4 2

Jonathan Cape, an imprint of Vintage,
20 Vauxhall Bridge Road,
London SW1V 2SA

Jonathan Cape is part of the Penguin Random House group of companies
whose addresses can be found at global.penguinrandomhouse.com.

Penguin
Random House
UK

Copyright© Raymond Briggs 2020

Raymond Briggs has asserted his right to be identified as the author of this Work
in accordance with the Copyright, Designs and Patents Act 1988

First published by Jonathan Cape in 2019

penguin.co.uk/vintage

A CIP catalogue record for this book is available from the British Library

ISBN 9781787331952

Colour separations by Altaimage Ltd
Printed and bound in China by C&C Offset Printing Co., Ltd

Penguin Random House is committed to a sustainable future for our business, our readers and our planet.
This book is made from Forest Stewardship Council® certified paper.

DÚN LAOGHAIRE-RATHDOWN LIBRARIES	
DLR27000053267	
BERTRAMS	25/11/2019
GP	02447848

Old age is a job with hard work and long hours
but you do get time off in the end.
ANON

"Maketh up a quote at ye beginning of they book;
'twill make people think thou art clever."
CHRISTOPHER MARLOWE, *The Obscure Tragedie*, Act II, Scene II

It is just as neurotic in old age
not to focus upon the goal of death
as it is in youth to repress fantasies
which have to do with the future.

CARL JUNG

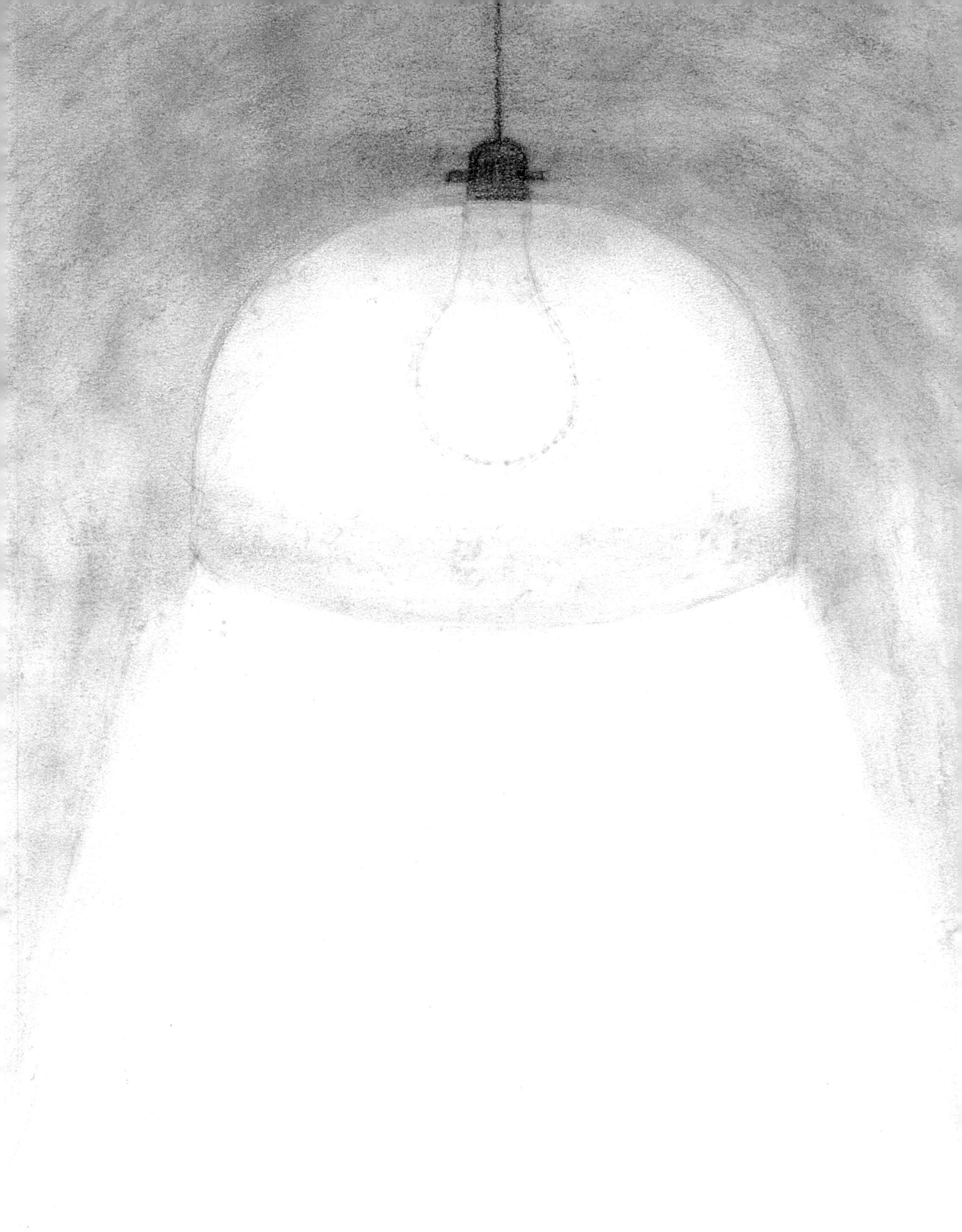

ALSO BY RAYMOND BRIGGS

Father Christmas

Fungus the Bogeyman

The Snowman

Gentleman Jim

When the Wind Blows

The Tin-Pot Foreign General and the Old Iron Woman

The Man

The Bear

Ethel & Ernest: A True Story

Fattypuffs and Thinifers

Ug: Boy Genius of the Stone Age

Notes from the Sofa

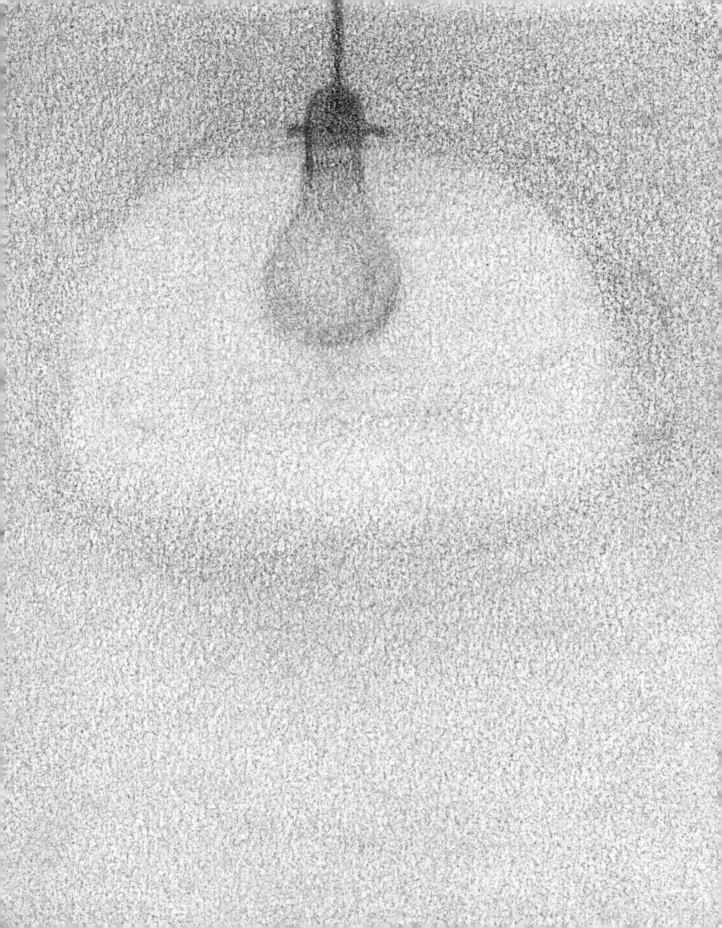

ACKNOWLEDGEMENTS

To Sue Thomson for her industry, endless patience and unfailing good humour.
John Vernon Lord for his interest, encouragement, books and music.

ONCE UPON A TIME

Once upon a time,
when we were young,
stories always began
"Once upon a time,"
then ended
"And they lived
happily ever after."
THE END

Now we are grown up,
stories no longer begin
"Once upon a time"
as
"Once upon a time"
is Now
and after
is not "ever after"
after all.

Happily or unhappily,
sooner or later,
it will be bedtime,
"Time for lights out"
and
THE END

The only good thing about old age
is that it doesn't last very long.
DAVID BAILEY

NOW

Old people are always
absorbed in something.
Usually themselves.

SIDNEY & BEATRICE WEBB

Whole load of stuff
to carry down . . .

break my neck
on these stairs one day . . .

old bones
snap like twigs . . .
two or three people I know
got osteoporosis . . .

Old age is upon us!
Even the wee's
Not what it was.

Seventy-one today!
Seventy-one today!
I've got the key of the morgue,
Never been seventy-one before

Be quiet!
You're frightening
the dog!

Besides,
you've been
seventy-one
for ages.

Key of the door . . .
Point is . . .
what is beyond
the door?

Shall I meet other wayfarers at night?
    Those who have gone before.
Then must I knock, or call when just in sight?
    They will not keep you standing at that door.

CHRISTINA ROSSETTI

Be careful, then, and be gentle about death.
For it is hard to die, it is difficult to go through the door
Even when it opens.

D.H. LAWRENCE

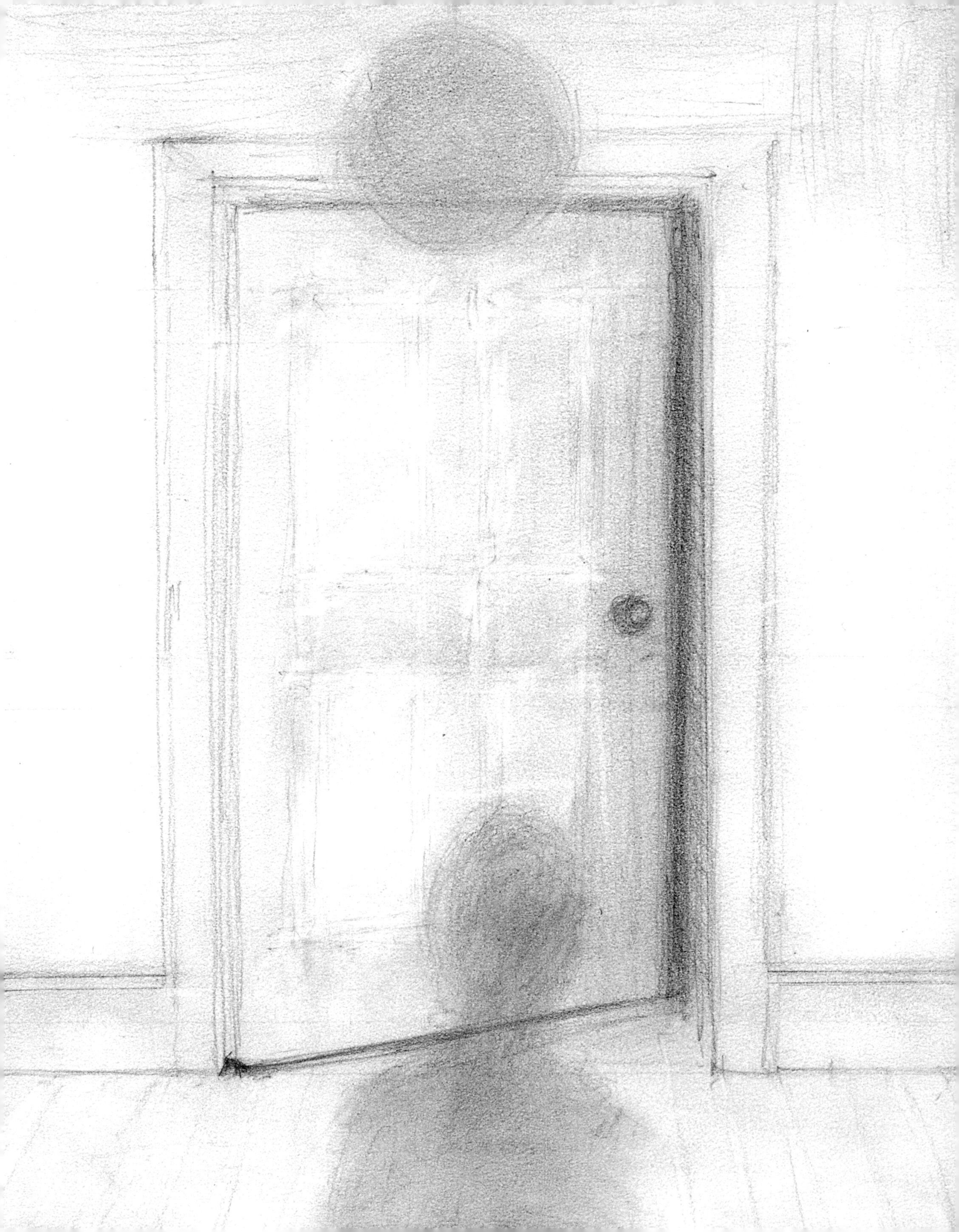

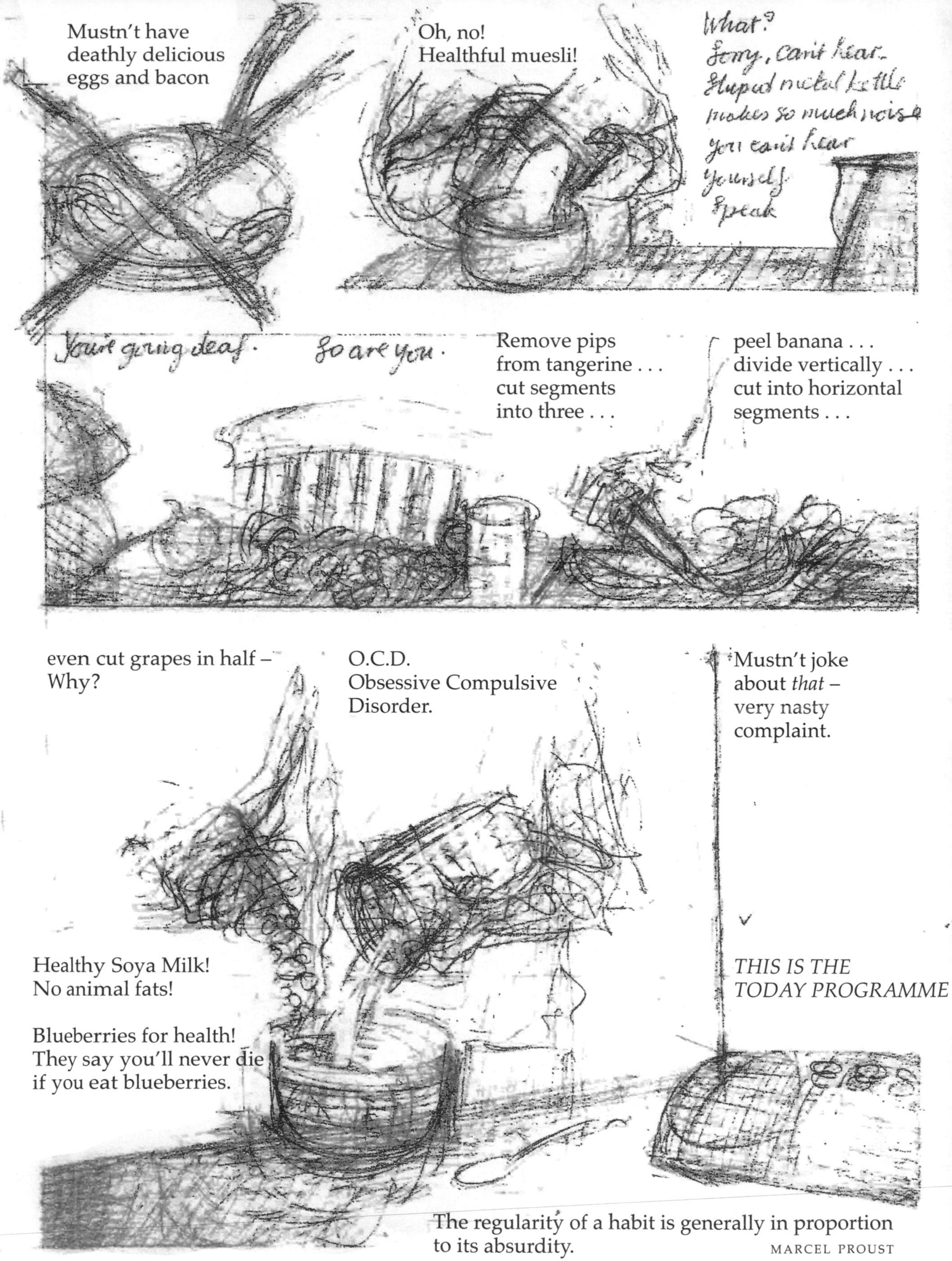
Mustn't have deathly delicious eggs and bacon
Oh, no! Healthful muesli!
What? Sorry, can't hear. Stupid metal kettle makes so much noise you can't hear yourself speak
You're going deaf.
So are you.
Remove pips from tangerine . . . cut segments into three . . .
peel banana . . . divide vertically . . . cut into horizontal segments . . .
even cut grapes in half – Why?
O.C.D. Obsessive Compulsive Disorder.
Mustn't joke about *that* – very nasty complaint.
Healthy Soya Milk! No animal fats!
Blueberries for health! They say you'll never die if you eat blueberries.
THIS IS THE TODAY PROGRAMME

The regularity of a habit is generally in proportion to its absurdity.
MARCEL PROUST

Cut crusts off bread for toast as slice is too big but also for aged and dummy teeth . . .

Divide into soldiers . . .
why are they called soldiers?
Because they get cut up
and smashed to bits?

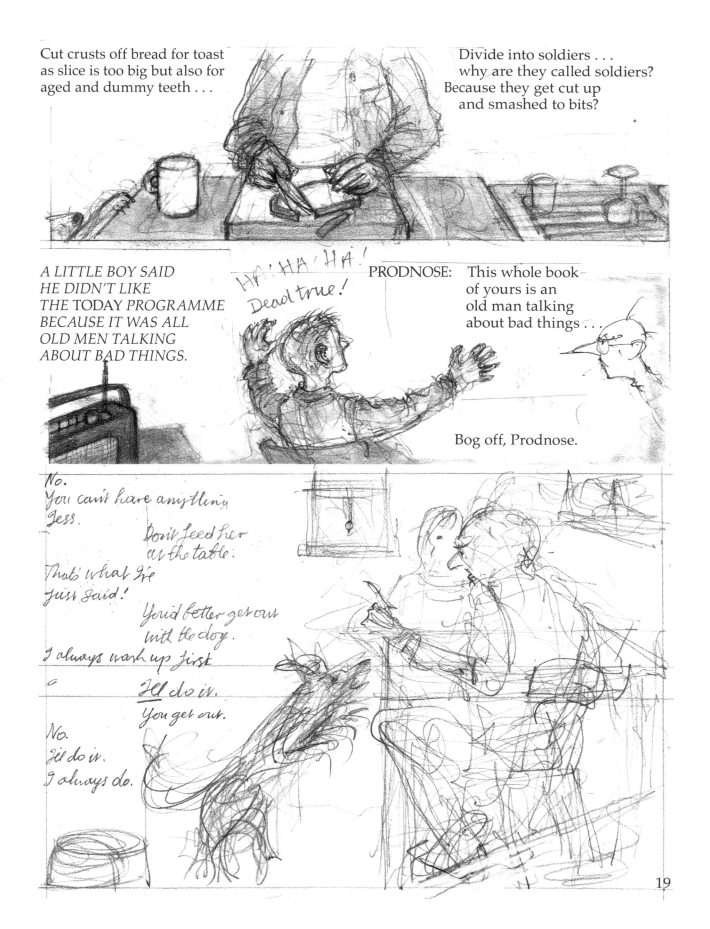

*A LITTLE BOY SAID
HE DIDN'T LIKE
THE* TODAY *PROGRAMME
BECAUSE IT WAS ALL
OLD MEN TALKING
ABOUT BAD THINGS.*

HA! HA! HA!
Dead true!

PRODNOSE: This whole book
of yours is an
old man talking
about bad things . . .

Bog off, Prodnose.

No.
You can't have anything
Jess.
        Don't feed her
        at the table.
That's what I've
just said!
        You'd better get out
        with the dog.
I always wash up first
        I'll do it.
        You get out.
No.
I'll do it.
I always do.

19

I'll make the bed.
You always do.
Aren't you always
tireder at breakfast?
You always do.

Come on, Jess.
Here we go —
yet another door...

What lies beyond?... ...
The Great Outdoors, Jess!
Come on!

SO, ARE ALL
RADIO COMEDY
WRITERS YOUNG?

OH, NO.
NOT AT ALL.
SOME OF THEM
ARE OVER THIRTY.

THIRTY!

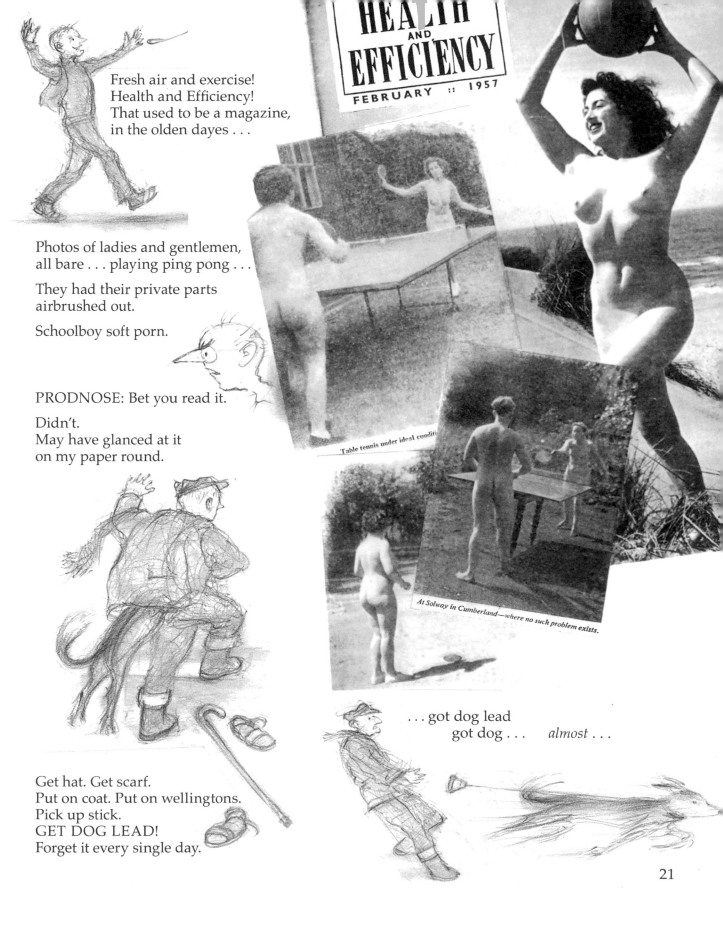

Fresh air and exercise!
Health and Efficiency!
That used to be a magazine,
in the olden dayes . . .

Photos of ladies and gentlemen,
all bare . . . playing ping pong . . .

They had their private parts
airbrushed out.

Schoolboy soft porn.

PRODNOSE: Bet you read it.

Didn't.
May have glanced at it
on my paper round.

HEALTH
AND
EFFICIENCY
FEBRUARY :: 1957

Table tennis under ideal conditi

At Solway in Cumberland—where no such problem exists.

. . . got dog lead
got dog . . .   almost . . .

Get hat. Get scarf.
Put on coat. Put on wellingtons.
Pick up stick.
GET DOG LEAD!
Forget it every single day.

CAMDEN CHEDDAR

I am not going deaf.
No. Not at all.
I am not in denial.
Young people today
just don't speak clearly.
   viz.
In our local restaurant,
a new waitress appears.
"Hullo," I say. "Haven't seen you before.
What's your name?"
"Camden," she says.
"Oh," I say. "How unusual.
Like Camden Town. Camden Lock?"
"No!" she shouts. "TAMSIN!"
   Typical.

Meeting our neighbour,
With her new dog,
I say, "What's his name?"
"Cheddar," she says.
"Oh," I say. "How unusual."
Patting its head,
"Hullo, Cheddar."
"No!" she shouts. "SHADOW!"
   You see?
It's not that I'm going deaf.
No. Not at all.
I am not in denial.
Young people today
just don't speak clearly.
It's pointless them denying it,
You can't hear what they say.
   Q.E.D.

Your Dim and Hollow Eyes methinks
the Loss of your Hearing, and the
Faltering of the rest of your Senses
should Mind ye, without more ado,
that Death has laid hold of ye already.

L'ESTRANGE, *Fables of Aesop*
1692, Fable 350

Nowadays, poor diction is everywhere; it even gets into our own family.

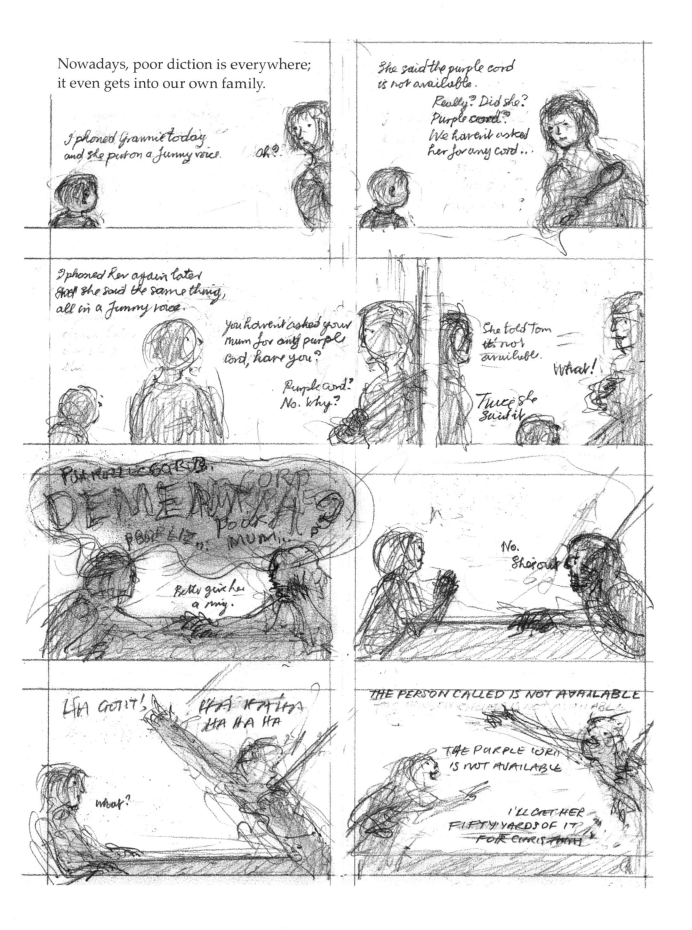

The poor diction has been spreading in recent years even to the elderly, even to Me and Her in Tesco last week.

Forgot post letters
letters in car

Letters put on dashboard
so not forget them

I would miss
this walk

Mustn't forget
post letters . . .

forgot them

But why should I
ever have to stop
doing it?

bad leg . . . ?
bad ankle . . . ?

arthritis . . . ?
loss of
balance . . . ?

loads of
reasons . . .

old folks
home . . . ?

Over my dead body.

Might get like that elderly gent
we saw last week . . .

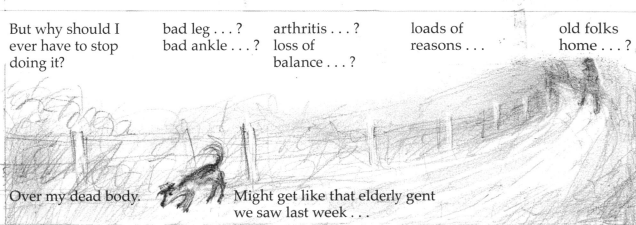

ELDERLY GENTLEMAN

As cars rush past him
the elderly gentleman
tall, dignified and military
steps out of the shop
and onto the pavement
his legs look crumpled
and not quite part of him
hesitant stick in hand
nervously watching the traffic
rushing past him
his legs working more or less
as part of him
leaning on his stick
he winces across the road
to his small red car
struggles to open the door
as cars rush past him
then collapses into his seat
clutching his stick
which is part of him
and drags his legs inside
like luggage.

THE LAST TIME

I walk this path every day.
One day, I know,
I will walk it for the last time.
How many other last times are there?
How many not remembered?

The last time you kissed your mother.
The last time you hugged your father.
The last time you made love
With someone.
The other unremembered last times –

The last time your little boy
Climbed onto your shoulders.
The last time your little girl
Wrapped her arms round your neck,
And cuddled you.

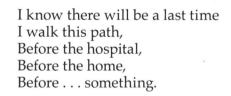

I know there will be a last time
I walk this path,
Before the hospital,
Before the home,
Before . . . something.

And the irony is
You never know,
At the time,
That it is to be
The last time.

Great clots of primroses
everywhere!
Never seen so many.

Queen Victoria's
favourite flower,
wasn't it?
Or Albert's.

Clusters of violets
on the bank.
Amazing deep colour.
Beautiful.

Good job this book's
not in colour.
I'd have to paint
the bloody things.

White violets, too.

Puff . . . puff . . .
phew!
Never used to notice
this little hill . . .

Thoughts of death
pile up to an astonishing
degree as the years increase.
Willy-nilly, the ageing person
prepares himself for death.
                    JUNG

puff . . .
    puff . . .

Hiya,
Willy!

Does the road wind uphill all the way?
            Yes, to the very end.
Will the day's journey take the whole day long?
            From morn to night, my friend.

Will there be beds for all who seek?
            Yea, beds for all who come.

                    CHRISTINA ROSSETTI

Very quiet just here.
A great feeling of peace.
Why is that?

The man who lived next to the
church said it was a very spiritual
place. Probably why the Christians
chose it for their church.

He's buried here now.
Good place to be buried.

The Victorians knew all about death.
They didn't try to pretend it never
happened, there was so much of it then.
When you look at the gravestones,
you realise most families suffered
the death of one or more children.

There is a tombstone for a couple
born in the 1820s. They both died in
their early sixties, but by then six of
their children had died. Benjamin
aged 22, Lucy 38, Anna 17,
Catherine 22, Enos 22, Mary aged
one year.
    The stone was erected by their
surviving sons and daughters.
    They must have been worried
when their twenty-second birthday
came round.

STRANGERS

For five years,
the famous man has lain
in a corner of the churchyard.
Weather has already worn away his stone.
Dates of birth and death are blurred.
Now, even his name has gone,
covered by lichens.
Once, it was up in lights,
now, even stone cannot keep it on.
A stranger would never learn
what famous man lay there,
just somebody,
some body,
another nameless stranger.

The gravestones in old churchyards often contain
many moving and tragic stories:

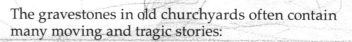

> Children of JOHN BEALE
> HANNAH died 1795 aged 6 months
> HANNAH died 1797 aged 5 months
> JOHN BEALE died 1801 aged 31

John Beale was twenty-five when his first baby died
and twenty-seven when his second baby died.
Four years later, he died.
His wife lost her husband and two children in six years.

> JANE wife of John Locke
> died 16 March 1897 aged 35
> FREDERICK son of John Locke
> died 27 March 1897 aged 14
> JOSEPH son of John Locke
> killed on Great Western Railway
> 1902 aged 17

Joseph was twelve when his brother of fourteen and his
mother of thirty-five died.
Mother and son died eleven days apart.
John Locke lost his wife and two sons in five years.

NAN

Lying in the churchyard,
on the rubbish dump,
ready for the bonfire,
a curious plastic framework.

I pick it up
and turn it over.
Dead, brittle stalks stick out
from plastic foam.

A framework of lines.

What can it be?
I turn it over.

Her loved and lettered name
already decaying,
her flowers long gone.

NAN
Her brittle stalks
dead and dried,
lying on the ground.

I set it on a shelf.
A reminder.
As if I needed one.

WESTERN PHILOSOPHY

Will I go to her funeral,
or will she go to mine?
Either way,
sure as hell,
I'm gonna be there,
dead or alive.

THE WIDOWED

If she should die
or if I die
one will remain
alone
once more
will have to choose a stone
once more
plant flowers on a grave
once more
and walk home
alone
too old now
for more
love.

WAR MEMORIAL

Every day, up by the church,
I pause by the War Memorial.
Nineteen Fourteen to Nineteen Eighteen
Burgess Cornford Cross
Dence Heaver Hunt
Stilwell Tetley Weaver
Weaver Welfare
Nineteen Thirty-Nine to Nineteen Forty-Five
Duke Funnel Pickering
Prescott Tetley
All from this small village,
died far away.

It's five months now,
since Poppy Day.
The flimsy British Legion wreath
lies propped against the cross,
plastic poppies stuck to cardboard.
Blown by wind and rain,
sometimes I find it,
far away.

High above,
silver pencils from the airport
soar through the blue
to holiday homes and sunshine,
far away.

Ah!   "and ever gently slopes downhill;"   no puffing!
Downhill home

"The path before you lies,
It is not hard to find, nor tread;
No rocks to climb, no lanes to thread;

But broad, and straight, and even still.
And ever gently slopes downhill . . . "

With courage seek the kingdom of the dead.

LEONIDAS OF TARENTUM
trans CHARLES MERIVALE

Saw a kingfisher
flash under this
bridge once.

There used to be
trout in the pool
here.

Swallows nested
in our garage
for over twenty years.

Once one swooped in
and brushed my cheek
as it flew past.

Oh, Jess!
SPLOSH! In she goes!
The water-mad dog.

You should have been
an otter, Jess.

ACROSS THE LANE

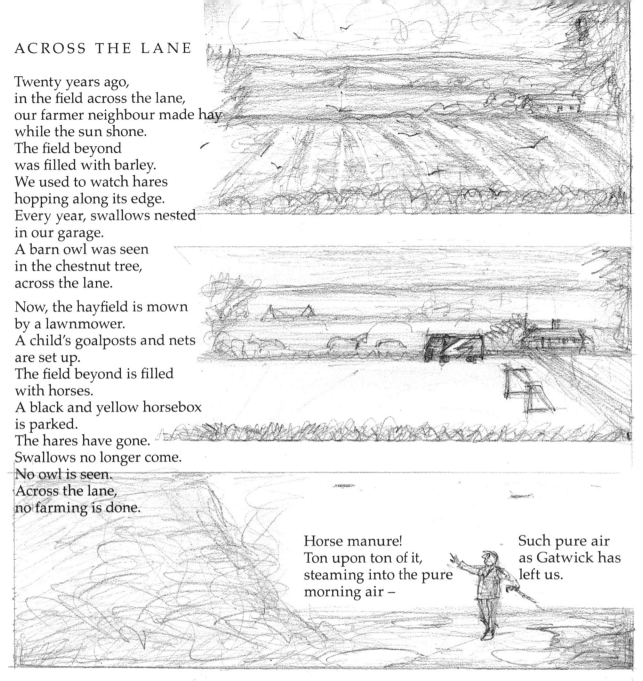

Twenty years ago,
in the field across the lane,
our farmer neighbour made hay
while the sun shone.
The field beyond
was filled with barley.
We used to watch hares
hopping along its edge.
Every year, swallows nested
in our garage.
A barn owl was seen
in the chestnut tree,
across the lane.

Now, the hayfield is mown
by a lawnmower.
A child's goalposts and nets
are set up.
The field beyond is filled
with horses.
A black and yellow horsebox
is parked.
The hares have gone.
Swallows no longer come.
No owl is seen.
Across the lane,
no farming is done.

Horse manure!
Ton upon ton of it,
steaming into the pure
morning air –

Such pure air
as Gatwick has
left us.

Just so that girlies
can trot about,
bouncing up and down
with their legs wide apart,

and with a huge
hairy animal
in between their thighs.

I wonder why
it's so popular?

I suppose the horse or pony
is the psychological bridge
which carries the pubescent
female from dollies and ballet
to the full-blown horror of
the spotty teenage male?

PRODNOSE:
Freud said the old are
jealous of the young.

I'm not jealous of a
spotty teenager!

No? Why not?
You're a spotty OAP.

Splodge off,
Prodnose.

Now children,
once upon a time,
there used to be
"Agri-cult-ure".

Write it down.

Fields produced
tons and tons
of potatoes,
wheat and barley . . .

Now there are
just horses producing
tons and tons of poo.

Mustn't turn into
a Grumpy Old Man . . .

Grumpy Old Men
are boring.

They are so boring
they put them on
the television.

I don't think I'm *really* grumpy.

I'm just clear-sighted –
with the clear-sightedness
born of age and experience . . .

Yes . . . that's it.
PRODNOSE: No it isn't it.

Today the world changes so quickly that in
growing up we take leave not just of youth, but
of the world we were young in . . . Fear and
resentment of what is new is really a lament for
the memories of our childhood.

PETER MEDAWAR
The Effecting of All Things Possible, 1969

Go up to car.

Get letters.

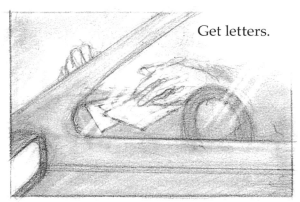

Don't drop letters in wet.

Don't forget the dog.

Don't go in road – certain death.

ANXIETY: TRAFFIC

Instead, hop over wall – easy . . .

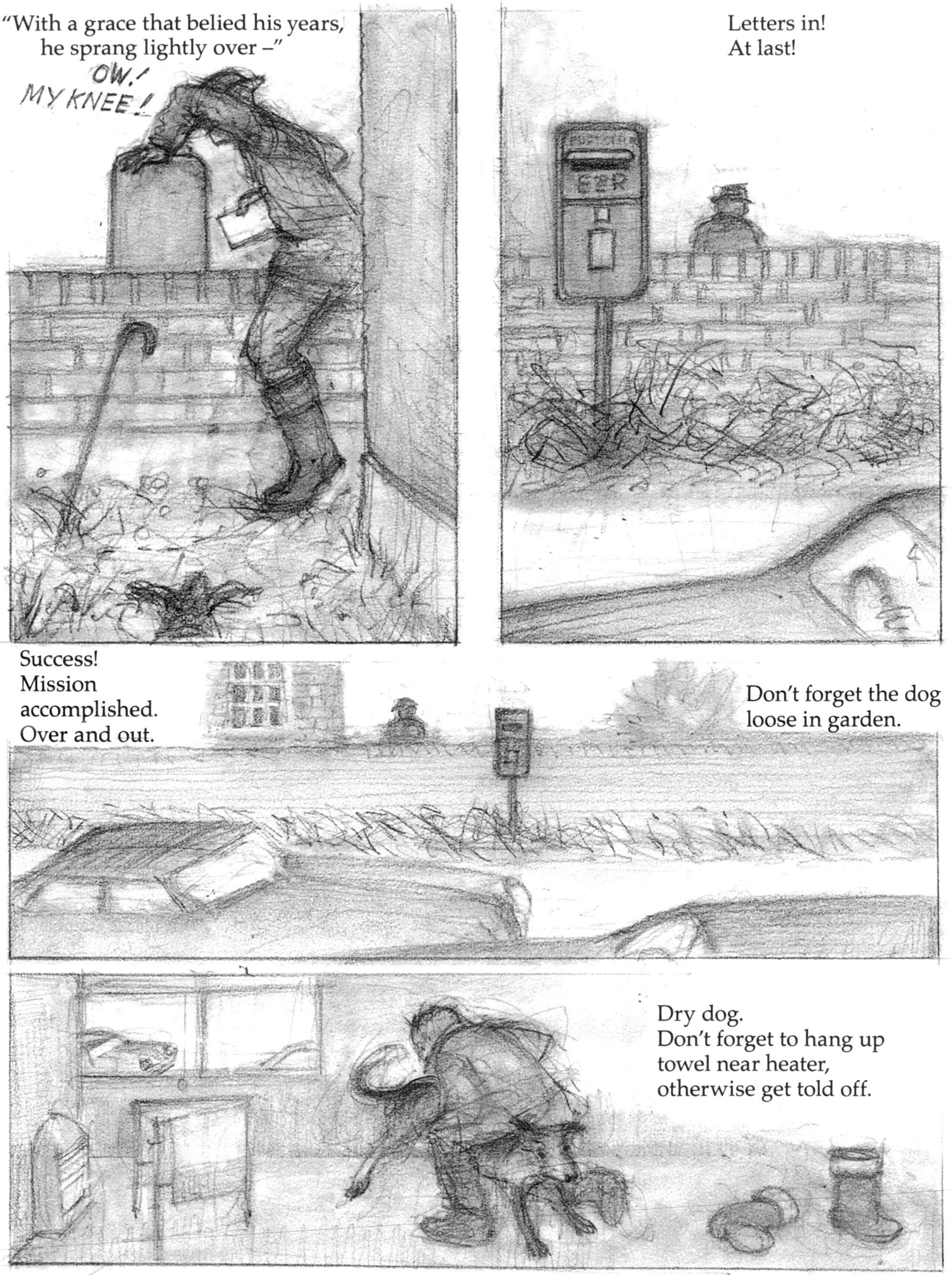
"With a grace that belied his years,
he sprang lightly over –"
OW! MY KNEE!
Letters in!
At last!
Success!
Mission
accomplished.
Over and out.
Don't forget the dog
loose in garden.
Dry dog.
Don't forget to hang up
towel near heater,
otherwise get told off.

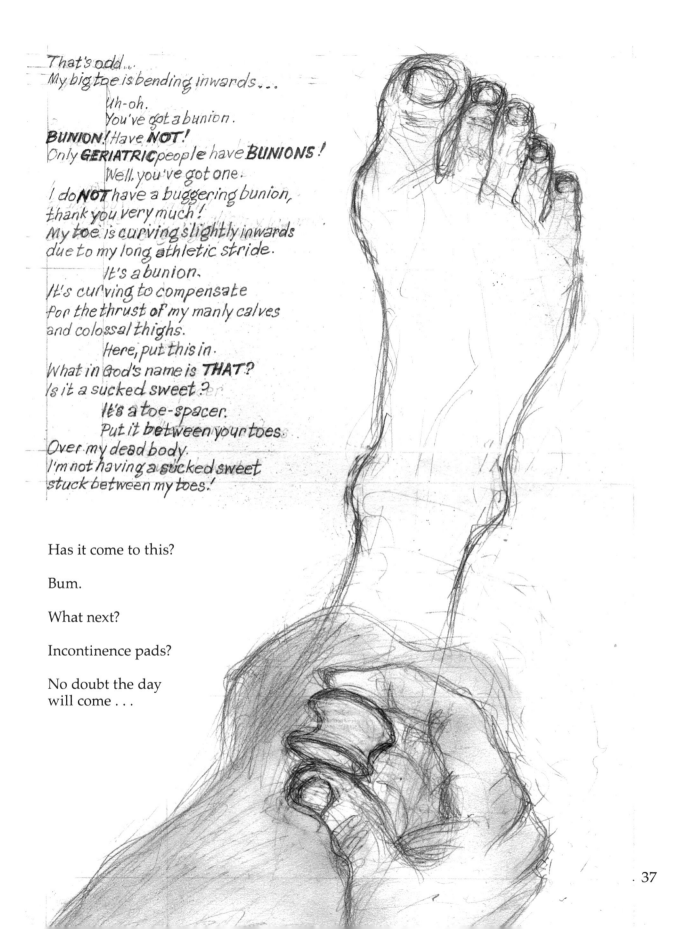

That's odd...
My big toe is bending inwards...

Uh-oh.
You've got a bunion.

BUNION! Have **NOT**!
Only **GERIATRIC** people have **BUNIONS**!

Well, you've got one.

I do **NOT** have a buggering bunion,
thank you very much!
My toe is curving slightly inwards
due to my long athletic stride.

It's a bunion.

It's curving to compensate
for the thrust of my manly calves
and colossal thighs.

Here, put this in.

What in God's name is **THAT**?
Is it a sucked sweet?

It's a toe-spacer.

Put it between your toes.

Over my dead body.
I'm not having a sucked sweet
stuck between my toes!

Has it come to this?

Bum.

What next?

Incontinence pads?

No doubt the day
will come . . .

37

Had them in hospital once,
after big op.
Three o'clock in the morning,
messed pyjama trousers.
Nurse happened to look in just then.
I said, "You'd better get me some sort of pad
if this is going to go on.
I need some baggy pants, too,
with this catheter thing stuck down my willy."
Also a rubber pipe was attached to the catheter,
then to a plastic bag on a pole on wheels.
So she came back with this enormous pad,
which I recognised as a Dr White's,
and a gigantic pair of paper pants
like old ladies' wartime bloomers.
I put the pad on and wrestled the bloomers
past the rubber pipe and catheter
and re-adjusted the post-op stockings:
white stockings which go right up the thighs.
Mine had purple borders at the tops;
quite saucy.
Suddenly, I thought, here I am
at three in the morning,
wearing women's fancy stockings,
old ladies' bloomers,
and with a Dr White's sanitary towel
stuck up my bum.

I cried.

The nurse came over and gave me a cuddle.

In the midst of this, to show my gratitude,
I put a hand on her thigh,
and thought afterwards I shouldn't have.

Still, you don't often get the chance
to be a dirty old man, do you?

PRODNOSE: You are a disgusting
                      old creep.

After the op, when I was lying in a semi-
anaesthetised stupor, a very glamorous, rather posh,
nurse stood by the bed and washed my penis for me.
"I do apologise," she said.
"Don't worry,"I said politely.
Why do these things only happen when you're OLD?

Sue's coming in a minute.

Oh, good. I need a quick slash

Don't talk like that when she's here. She's very sensitive.

I'm talking about a haircut.

Now listen, Sue. I don't like it tumbling all over my shoulders. When I toss my head the red-gold highlights Flash all round the room.
It disturbs other people in restaurants. But don't cut too much off the top. There's not much there.

I'll try and make the most of what there is.

4½ MINUTES LATER

All these bits of grey fluff . . .

It's got no body. It's like cotton wool, without the vitality of cotton wool.

It's muck. It's detritus. It's DEAD.

WHAT CAN THIS MEAN?

PRODNOSE: Shall I spell it out for you?   NO!

Only five letters . . . NO!

Lucky to have *any*.
At least there is some.

It's not dead and *gone*.
Just dead.

The birds will like it
for their nests.

"I wonda where
de boidies is . . ."

There's the robin already.

"De spring is sprung, De grass is riz . . ."

De spring is in de air, Even if it ain't in de hair –

SUSSEX OAP BACKS FLUFF RECYCLING SCHEME
"Our wildlife needs our fluff," says silver-haired
pensioner.

ON HIS BALDNESS

At dawn I sighed to see my hairs fall:
At dusk I sighed to see my hairs fall.
For I dreaded the time when the last lock should go . . .
They are all gone and I do not mind at all!

PO CHU-I *c* 834 AD
trans Arthur Waley

PRODNOSE: You're rambling again.

Be off, Prodnose.
You couldn't get into the papers.

I was with Mr Beachcomber
for over forty years!

OLD MEN'S HAIR

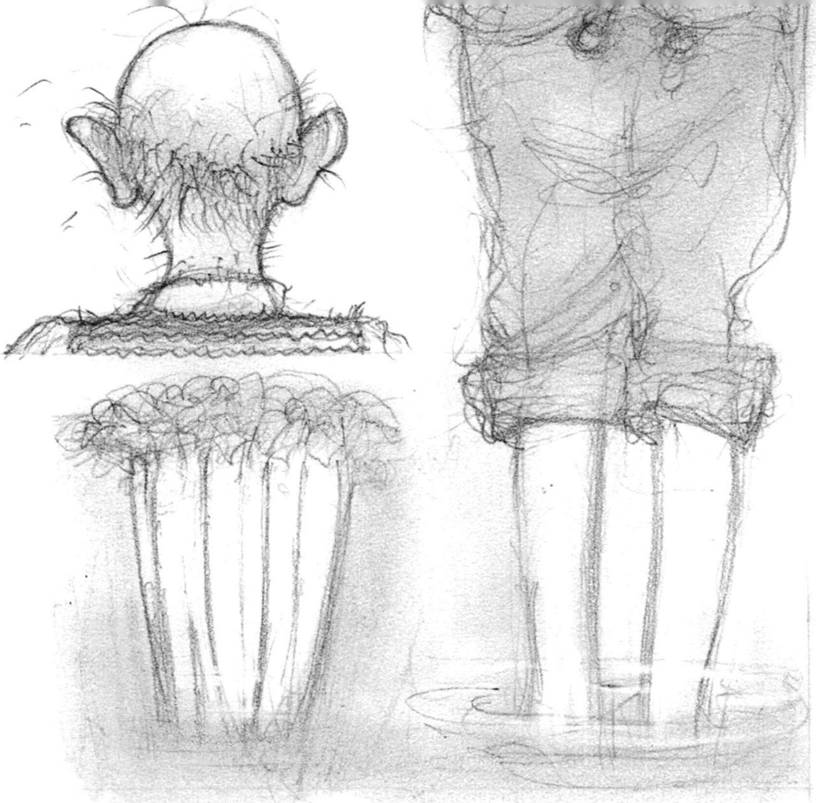

When you're old
Why does hair go bad?
Head hair
goes grey
goes white
falls out
disappears

Leg hair
just disappears
Little girl said,
"Old men's legs are like celery."

Eyebrows
go mad
an inch a week
can't see out
unsafe driving
comb and cut
like a fringe

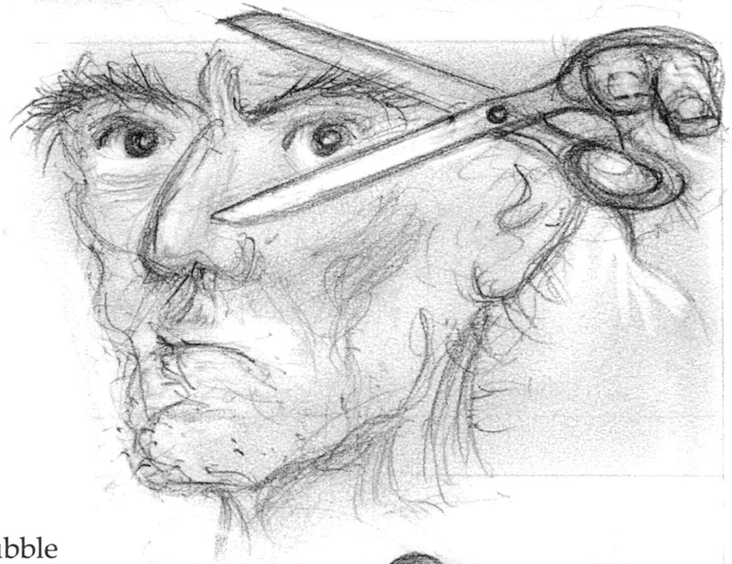

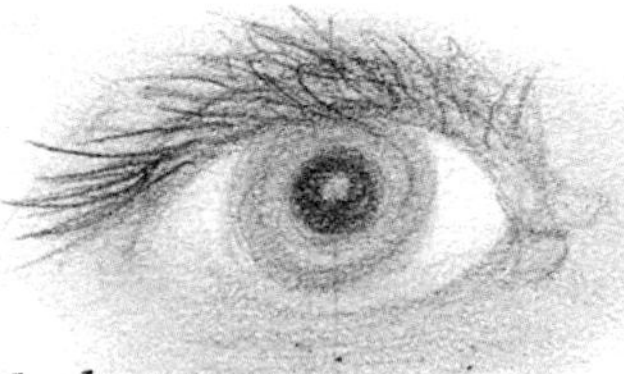

Eyelashes
no change
long lustrous
entrancing as ever
Beard
no change
rugged designer stubble
as ever

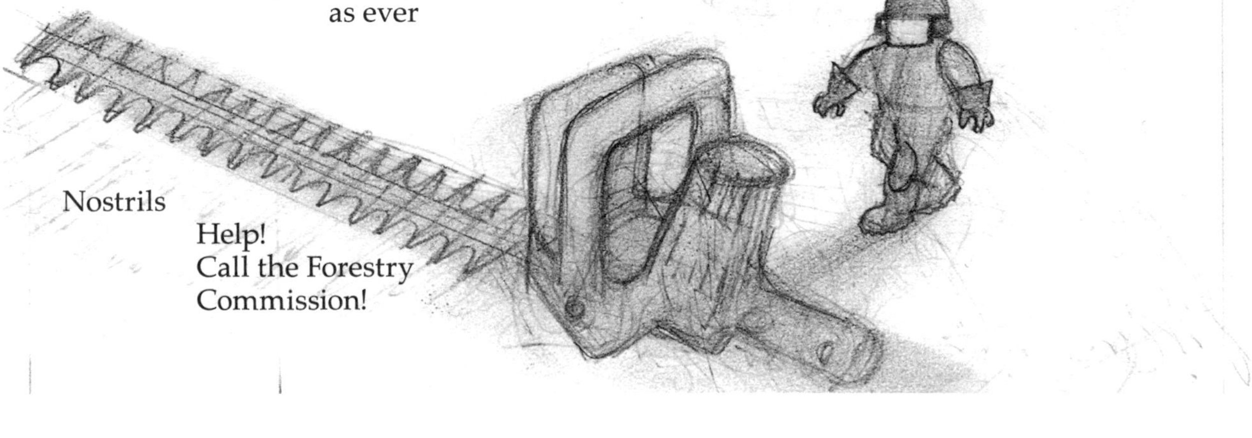

Nostrils
Help!
Call the Forestry
Commission!

When you're old,
first thing you look at
in the paper is the
Obituaries page . . .

See who's in and who's out.
Never mind the Test score.
See who's dead
and who's still battling on . . .

and whether
they're older or younger
than you are.

OBITUARY

A man of letters.
Humour.
Tumour.
        A difference
of one letter.
One made him better,
One brought a letter.
What a difference
one letter can make.

Here we go –
Ah! Born 1936,
two years younger than me.
Ha!

PRODNOSE: Surely that makes you
feel *more* vulnerable?

No! Twerp!
I've beaten
him.

Yes, but if those *younger*
than you are already
dying . . .

Shut up, Prodnose.

Here's another one –
born 1947!
Blimey.
After the War!
Died at fifty-eight.
Oh well . . . rock star.
Say no more.

Now, here's a good one –
Born 1905.
Died exactly one hundred.
Terrific.

        Shows it can be done.
A really good innings.

Do you want
to live to be
100?

I suppose not . . .
not really . . .
no.

You have had daily Examples
of Mortality before your Eyes,
in all People of all Sorts, Ages,
        and Degrees;
and is not the Frequent Spectacle
    of other People's Deaths,
a Memento sufficient to make
    you think of your Own?

So what age would you
like to die at?
72 too early?
100 too late?

So, what shall
we say?
75 suit you?

Just die,
Prodnose!

L'ESTRANGE,
Fables of Aesop, 1692

Yes, Mr Aesop, it does make you think of your own.

THE AGE OF DEATH
of Sixty Cartoonists & Illustrators

UNDER 40 YEARS

Graham Laidler (PONT)	32
Paul Crum	36
Gerard Hoffnung	27
Phil May	39
Timothy Birdsall	27

40–50 YEARS

Tom Browne	40
Randolph Caldecott	40

50–60 YEARS

Mark Boxer	57
Robert Sherriffs	54
Frank Bellamy	59
Herbert Foxwell	53
Victor Weisz (VICKY)	53
Kate Greenaway	55

60–70 YEARS

Russell Brockbank	66
Michael ffolkes	63
William Sillince	68
William Pett	69
Roy Wilson	65
Dudley Watkins	62
Linley Sambourne	66
Sidney Strube	64
Mel Calman	63
Charles Keene	68

70–80 YEARS

Arthur Rackham	72
Thomas Rowlandson	70
Edward Ardizzone	79
Heath Robinson	72
Frank Reynolds	77
Mary Tourtel	74
David Low	72
Philip Zec	74
Joseph Lee	74
Carl Giles	79
Osbert Lancaster	78
Michael Cummings	78
Leslie Illingworth	77
Beatrix Potter	77
Leslie Wood (SPY)	71
George Stampa	76
Tom Webster	76
George Belcher	73
Bruce Bairnsfather	72
Kenneth Bird (FOUGASSE)	78
Nicolas Bentley	71
John Glashan	72

80–90 YEARS

Bert Thomas	83
Donald McGill	87
Rowland Emett	84
Austin Payne	80
Reg Smythe	81
Bernard Partridge	84
Max Beerbohm	84
John Millar Watt	80
H. M. Bateman	83
John Hassall	80

OVER 90 YEARS

Douglas Mays	91
Alfred Bestall	93
John Tenniel	94
E. H. Shepard	97
Kathleen Hale	102

Under 40 years FIVE
40 – 50 years TWO
50 – 60 years SIX
60 – 70 years TEN
70 – 80 years TWENTY-TWO
80 – 90 years TEN
Over 90 years FIVE

Certainly, dying in the seventies seems to be by far the most popular, so it is the most likely decade for departure.

Almost half of them died before the age I am now, so I am already lucky to be alive.

The mathematical average is sixty-nine, so I've already passed that. WAH! HEY! I'm above average!

Smug git!

Conceited prick!

PRODNOSE: Tee Hee
Any the wiser?

Here – this is good.

TEN CHARACTERISTICS OF OLD AGE
How do you rate?

1. **RIGID IN ADHERING TO ROUTINES OF DAILY LIFE?**
    Can't answer this now – four minutes *past* five!
    Late for tea.

2. **ARE YOUR THOUGHTS TINGED WITH PESSIMISM?**
    Don't know about "tinged" . . .

3. **DIFFICULTY IN DECISION MAKING?**
    Not sure whether to answer that or not.

4. **UNABLE TO THINK OF, OR DO, TWO THINGS AT ONCE?**
    I thought I had a cup of tea somewhere . . .
    I *did* make it, didn't I?

5. **BLUNTING OF FEELING? APATHY, INDIFFERENCE?**
    Who *cares* about the tea?
    Who cares the world is getting hotter? I'll be gone soon.

6. **RESISTANT TO CHANGE?**
    Who wants change? Things can only get worse.

7. **LACK OF SPONTANEITY?**
    Yes, thank God. Lack of spontaneity has kept me
    out of all sorts of trouble.

8. **GREATER CAUTION?**
    It's being cautious that stops life-threatening spontaneity.

9. **INCREASED ANXIETY?**
    He who is not anxious has no imagination.*

10. **DISTRUST OF THE UNFAMILIAR?**
    Well, of course. You don't know where they've been.

    * Briggs

"People who are anxious and pessimistic
are more likely to get dementia," it says.

Hey ho! So that's one more thing
to get anxious and pessimistic about.

Nevertheless . . . I'm not apathetic
about *everything* . . .

PRODNOSE: More's the pity

ON HEARING THE FIRST
NIGHTINGALE IN SPRING

In the spring time,
a young man's fancy
turns to love,
while the old man
just loves fancying.

Walking across the fields,
we met a host of lovely girls,
laughing, friendly faces,
wild child eyes,
with backpacks and bedrolls.
Innocence abroad in Sussex.

Dirty old man abroad in Sussex,
surging teenage T shirts,
combat trouser thighs,
cuddly muddy boots,
backpacks and bedrolls
backpacks and bedrolls
the two-backed beast rolls.

Impure thoughts.

Then, out of the sun and laughter
into the shade of a wood
flooded with bluebells,
where we heard
the first nightingale of spring.

The pure song,
the haze of blue,
purified my thoughts

For a minute or two.

They said they were
on the Duke of Edinburgh's.
Lucky old him.
Wish they were on mine.

Come on, stop ogling.
You'll be late for
your precious tea

Or that morning last year driving into Brighton . . .

MORNING RUSH

morning
rush
hour
in
car
queuing
crawling
bored

clack
clack
clack
nearer
nearer

blouse
bursting
legs
legs
breasts

crawl
stop
wait
crawl
stop
wait

suddenly

woman

tall
legs

down in the driving seat
something stirred

clack
clack

clack
near

fishnet
legs
skirt
short
heels
high
hair
black

now

just
across
close

makeup
pancake
thick
pink
lips
thick

neck
thick
jaw
big
ankles
scrawny
calves
muscly
knees
knobbly

stubble

stubble
blue
pancake
thick
pink
stubble
blue

man

what a drag

48

Despite the increasing apathy,
as you get older, you become more intolerant,
more right-wing. Young Socialists become Tories,
young Tories become Fascists.

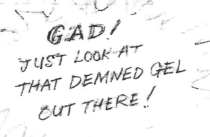

COLONEL BLIMP

Riding past my window,
a fat girl slumps in the saddle,
like a slummock on a sofa.
Jodhpur belly bulging
over jodhpur jelly thighs.
Fag in one hand,
phone in the other,
nattering, tittering,
cloud of smoke around her face,
the reins somewhere or other.

Living in a better world,
the horse retains its dignity,
just.
I lose mine,
and feel like Colonel Blimp.

Ah, the Property Page . . . the so-called property ladder,
another marker of Life Time.

HOUSEY HOUSEY
A Popular Game for All Ages

This little flat of yours is fine for us *now*,
but if we ever had a baby . . .

Yes, it's still *just about* all right,
but when she starts toddling about . . .

It's really impossible here!
They need a *garden* to play in –
swing, sandpit, paddling pool . . .

At last! We can get them outside.
But we'll need another bedroom soon.
It's difficult with them sharing that tiny room.

We'll *have* to move.
Bigger house – four beds if poss.
Then I can get down to some serious gardening –
vegetables, greenhouse, pond, fruit trees . . . Bliss!

We'd better build on, *if* we can afford it!
Ideally, they should all have a room *each*,
with A-Levels coming up.

The house seems so empty, so quiet.
I come in from work, close the front door,
and there's silence.
Not a sound. Not a soul.

This place is far too big for us.
Expensive to maintain and, quite honestly,
the garden is a bit of a burden.

We really need somewhere smaller –
less housework, less decorating.
I've had my fill of DIY,
and the garden is just impossible.

5

Two-bed bungalow –
little patio garden . . .
Near the shops. That's us!
Don't like driving these days.

6

Now I'm on my own, I don't need all this.
Least of all, a blessed garden!
A little one-bed flat would suit me fine,
like I had when I started out.

Can't get up the stairs now.
Locked myself out the other day!
Then when the stupid kitchen curtains
caught fire, I fell over and broke my wrist.

They say they'll find somewhere for me.
Nothing grand. Nice warm room.
Three meals a day. No shopping,
no cooking, no housework, no gardening,
no kids!

7

                    Paradise!

COMING HOME

The lights of our house
are out
my key grates into the lock
sounding too loud
too hollow
the door opens
I pause
listening to nothing
and no one
no music
no shouting calling
bounding down the stairs
they've gone
the door closes
another hollow sound
in the stillness
I stand
coat on
bag in hand
staring at someone
in the mirror
listening to the emptiness

In old age, you are constantly trying
to make good resolutions,
usually to do with trying
to live a bit longer.
You also have to bear
the irritating fads and fancies
of the young.

BOTTLE BANK

Smash bash crash
goes the glass
Smash bash crash

Green for red
Clear for white

Smash bash crash

Did we really drink
all that last night?

All that wine?
All that poison?

It's just not on

Feel fairly fit
just a bit off
Better lay off it
for a bit

Must just pop off
to the offy now
they've got
an offer on

DEAR GIRLIES
An Open Letter

With a mobile phone
you
    are never alone
    but being alone
            is good for
                    you
    never being alone
            is bad for
                    you
you
    may grow up
    empty
    filling the void
    of your mind
    with a phone
                cuts
                    you
        off from
                    you
        but maybe
                    you
want to be cut off from
                    you
    if someone phones
                    you
    if someone phones
            only
                    you
                    can answer

53

Also, with Old Age
come the endless PILLS.

SIDE EFFECTS

Your medicine may cause:

    dry mouth
    weakness
painful muscles
    muscle weakness
back pain
general pain
stomach pain
    swelling of feet
    low blood pressure
    slow heart rate
    loss of appetite
constipation
diarrhoea
    feeling sick
    being sick
indigestion
heartburn
    wind
    cough
    wheeze
    chest infection
skin rash
itching
swelling
    pain on passing urine
    blood in urine
    tiredness

sleepiness
sleeplessness
    runny nose
    rhinitis

painful persistent erection of penis
blimey
weight gain
    faintness
    dizziness
    tremor
tingling in hands
enlargement of breasts in men
blimey
    low white blood cells
easy bruising
easy bleeding
nose bleeds
    jaundice
    hepatitis
    bile disorder
hair loss
noise in ears

    agitation
    anxiety
    depression

(may be caused by
reading this leaflet)

CCTV

Queuing for the till
in the village shop,
I look up at the new camera –
a blurred image,
black and white,
back view,
of some old bloke,
just a head, a shirt, and trousers.
Couldn't see his face,
but you could tell
he was old,
really old.
Who was it?
Haven't seen anyone
in here like that . . .
mostly young mums,
crumpet in sun tops.
No one so decrepit.
I turn to look around,
and the blurred old git
also turns –

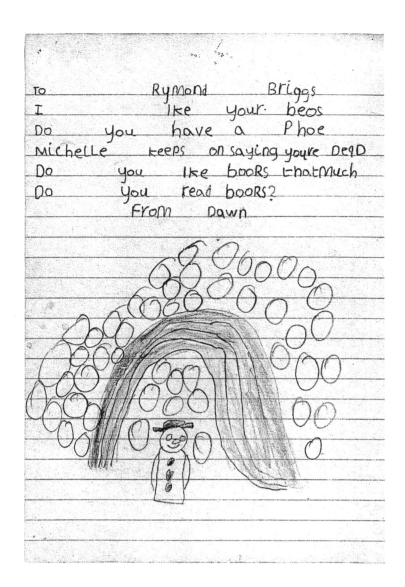

In old age the question of identity makes you as self-conscious as a teenager. Who are you? WHAT are you?
Someone said, "At twenty you worry about what people think about you.
At forty you don't care about what people think about you.
At sixty you realise they've not been thinking about you at all."
Usually, by seventy, they have completely forgotten about you.
A few ask "Is he still alive?" Others think you are already dead.
Sometimes you begin to wonder yourself.

I.D.	SURVEILLANCE RHYME

<table>
<tr><td></td><td>identity</td><td>BEE EN SIX</td></tr>
</table>

I.D.

               identity
               identity
               identity
What is your identity?
Have you any identification?
Have you got an identikit?
i.e. identity card
               identity number
               identity discs?
You must go on an identity parade
So you can identify yourself
If dead you can be identified by
Your dentition
Are you now, or have you ever been
A member of the identity party?
Have you ever been a victim of identity theft?
Have you ever had an identity crisis?
Have you ever met your own identity in the street?
Is he identical to you?
If not

               what's he look like?

SURVEILLANCE RHYME

BEE EN SIX

ATE EX GEE

AR A WYE

EM O EN DEE

And they have got
Your mar
        ket
        ing
        pro
        file

        bum

If a company has your first name
and your postcode, they can write
a fairly accurate marketing profile
of you. Your first name indicates
your age. The postcode tells them
your house and probable income.

I am not I
      I am this one
Walking beside me whom I do not see

JUAN RAMÓN JIMÉNEZ

CHINA IN A BULL SHOP

Waiting in Reception
at the garage,
body-builder man
behind the counter,
black sleeveless vest,
writhing tattoo biceps,
earrings and shaven head,
friendly grin. Nice bloke.
Three mechanics
on the bench behind me,
muscles, mugs of tea,
vests, boots, tattoos,
bullet heads, black grease
and sweat,
laughing.

I stand in their midst,
skinny and old,
educated and artistic,
pastel pink shirt,
long sleeves buttoned
to conceal spaghetti arms,
creamy summer trousers,
pale bare feet in sandals,
wispy white hair,
half moon spectacles
hanging from tendonous neck,
trying not to talk too posh,
feeling like an antique
piece of china
in a bull pen.

RURAL RETIREMENT

He is now blind,
and his wife cannot drive,
but every week, he polishes the car
he can no longer see.
And every afternoon,
between two and five,
he is banished to the caravan.

She retires to her bedroom mirrors,
hair, make-up, clothes and shoes.
In her colonial youth,
she was a beauty,
"The toast of the Veldt."

On the panelling in his caravan
is a newspaper pin-up.
A long-legged glamour girl
lolling on a beach,
her legs stretched astride the surf.

Later, when his wife picks her way
along the lane to the church,
in pale blue twinset and pearls,
she peers down at the ground,
setting each toe carefully,
as if tiptoeing through broken glass.
Outdoors, her make-up is a garish mask.

The drinking water jug they use
is green with slime.
She must know. She can see it.
He can't see it. He doesn't know.
Why is she punishing him?
What has he done?
How long ago?

CULTURAL CROSSROADS

At the village crossroads,
cars, vans and trucks,
noise and traffic signs –
     KEEP LEFT
     GIVE WAY
     NO ENTRY

The animals silently appear,
bullocks, cows and calves,
ambling peacefully along, unattended,
their big blue eyes oblivious, content.

Whilst vibrating traffic waits,
one stops to sniff, leisurely,
at the catseyes
in the middle of the road.

They wander on, at ease,
through the crossroads,
unhurried, at home
in their own calm world,
while exhausts fume
and engines throb.

As he moves away,
dignified and slow,
the catseyes bullock
arches his tail
in a graceful curve,
and drops five piles
of steaming dung
all through the crossroads.

Bullocks to you,
he seems to say.

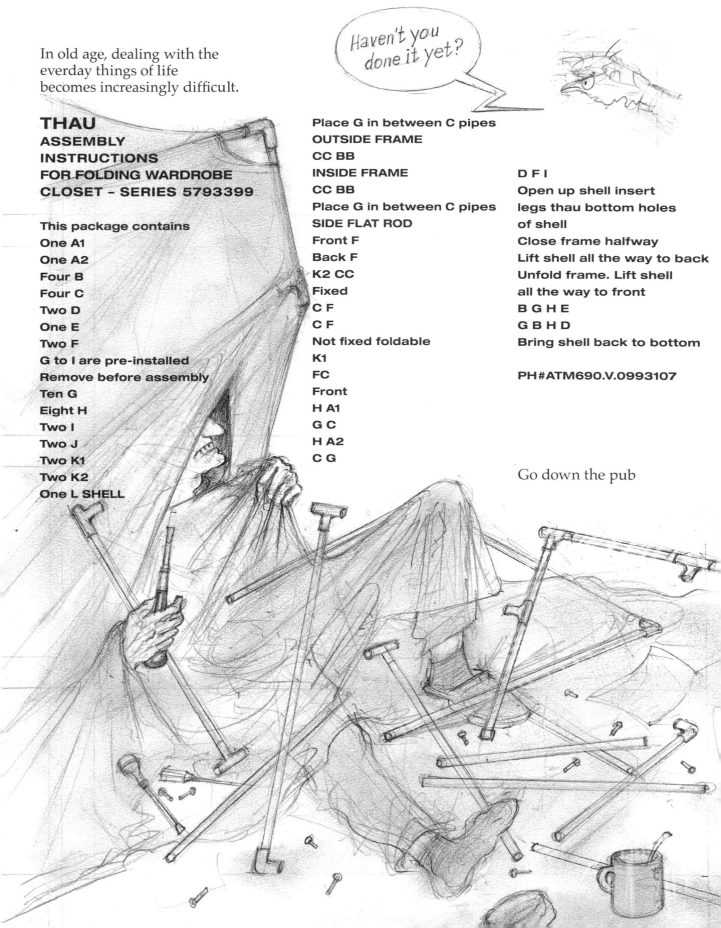

In old age, dealing with the everday things of life becomes increasingly difficult.

THAU
ASSEMBLY
INSTRUCTIONS
FOR FOLDING WARDROBE
CLOSET – SERIES 5793399

This package contains
One A1
One A2
Four B
Four C
Two D
One E
Two F
G to I are pre-installed
Remove before assembly
Ten G
Eight H
Two I
Two J
Two K1
Two K2
One L SHELL

Place G in between C pipes
OUTSIDE FRAME
CC BB
INSIDE FRAME
CC BB
Place G in between C pipes
SIDE FLAT ROD
Front F
Back F
K2 CC
Fixed
C F
C F
Not fixed foldable
K1
FC
Front
H A1
G C
H A2
C G

D F I
Open up shell insert
legs thau bottom holes
of shell
Close frame halfway
Lift shell all the way to back
Unfold frame. Lift shell
all the way to front
B G H E
G B H D
Bring shell back to bottom

PH#ATM690.V.0993107

Go down the pub

Combination DVD and VC...

Numeric buttons

Remote commander

① (DVD) OPEN/CLOSE button, (VCR...
) VCR SELECT button
① (DVD, VCR) NUMBER button, (VCR...
  button
④ SYSTEM button (This button is not...
⑤ SETUP button
⑥ (DVD, VCR) MOVE/SELECT in OSD,...
  Up/Down button
⑦ (DVD) TITLE/PBC button
⑧ (DVD) AUDIO LANGUAGE Select,...
  button
⑨ (DVD) SUBTITLE Select button
⑩ REVERSE SEARCH button
⑪ PLAY/PAUSE button
⑫ (DVD) PREVIOUS button (move into a...
  or track)
⑬ (VCR) Record SPEED button
⑭ (VCR) Record button
⑮ (VCR) TV/VCR button

Power
Display
Title
Zoom
Select
Arrow buttons
Play/Pause
Skip/Frame
Audio
Subtitle
Program
Repeat

⑯ 3D button
⑰ CM SKIP
⑱ Replay button
⑲ POWER button
⑳ DVD SELECT button
㉑ (VCR) INPUT Selection bu...

Remote Control

Seven weeks ago, a DVD player and a digital box were installed. The man gave us two more remote controls and swiftly showed us how simple it all was. There are now 108 buttons.

Then yesterday, whilst fiddling about, a flap on our first remote control accidentally opened and 21 more were revealed, 129 buttons in all.

Apart from the original 6 buttons: ON OFF 1 2 3 4 and VOL, for seven weeks none of the others have been used.

We can't remember what the man said and can't face reading the 148 pages of instructions. We are too old. We are running out of life time.

There is a similar array of buttons and lights in the car. The manual for the sound system alone is 38 pages, while the manual for the car itself is 239 pages. In all, 277 pages.

Who has got the time? Not me at 71, thank you. If this is the way the world is going, it's not worth volunteering for euthanasia but it's definitely time to get off.

We haven't the time to take our time.

EUGENE IONESCO

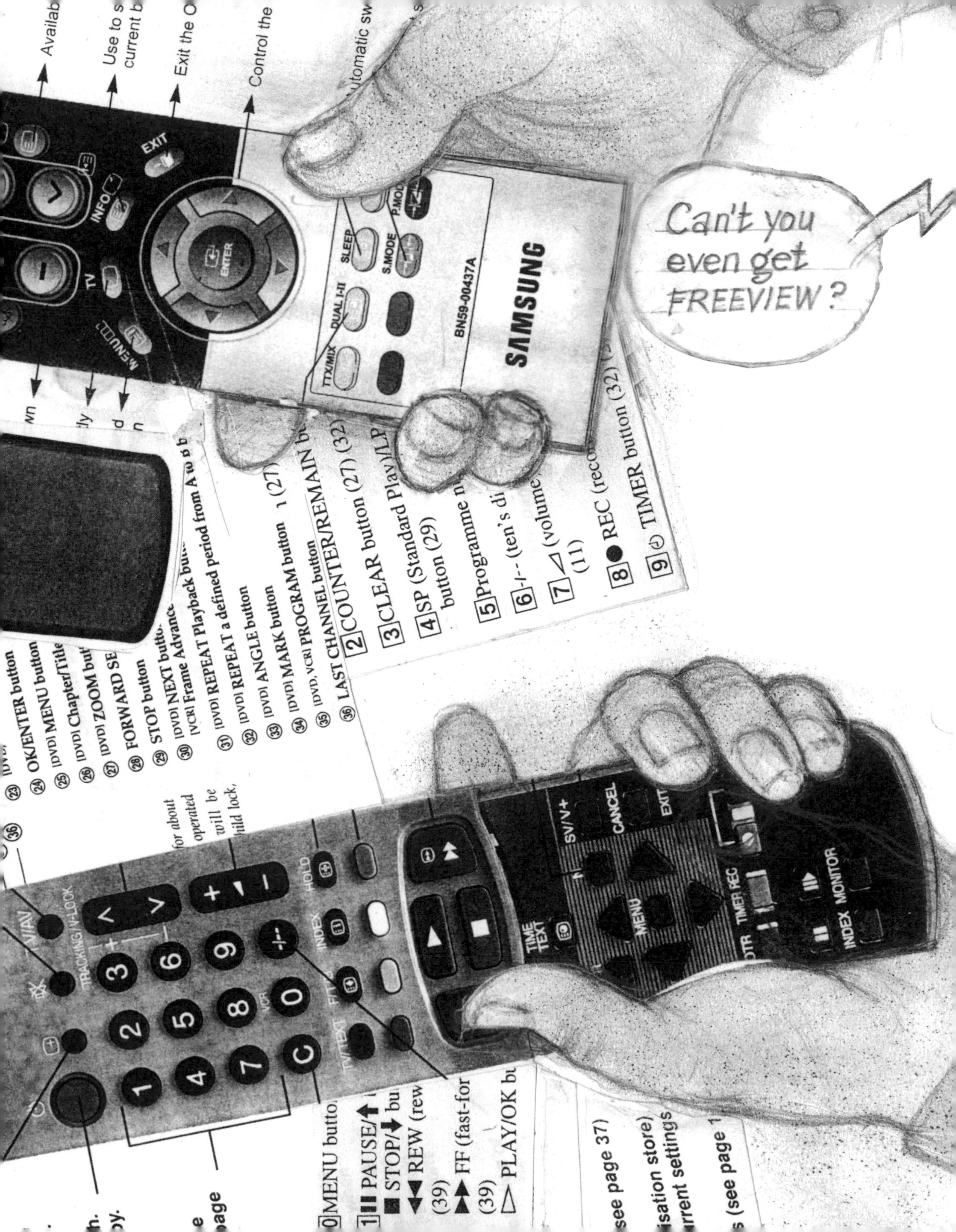
Can't you even get FREEVIEW?

There are all the things
you always wanted
to do but never had
the time. Now there
is endless spare time . . .

Retired people all say they
wonder how they ever had time
to go to work.

PLUM GLUT

Damson tree,
laden.
Blue-black plums,
mellow mauve bloom,
green-gold flesh.
An abundance
of plums.

Too many to eat,
wicked to waste.
Make jam?
Never have
made jam.
Always meant to
make jam.

How to do it?
Boil it?
Bake it?
Wicked to waste it.
Waste not plums.
Want not plums.
Want jam.

How much time
jam take to make?
Jars!
Got get jars.
Jam jars,
pots, pans,
jam pans.

Pectin!
Remember . . . "Pectin?"
Ancient aunt – "Pectin."
Damn good jam.
What godsname Pectin?
Better get
PECTIN in.

Got go shop,
get ten tins Pectin.
Got go shop,
get two tons sugar.
Got go shop,
get big wood spoons.
Jam tomorrow!

Poxy Pectin jam not set!
Jam, set and match
to Pectin.
Give in.
Goddam Damson Jam!
Got get shop jam.
Go Tesco.

ROSE GARDEN

This afternoon,
a single shot.
Cawing in panic,
crows flock from the trees.
My neighbour,
shooting garden pests.
Minutes later, I call round
with a leaflet about roses.
"Come and look at this," he says.
"It will amuse you –
a rabbit and a squirrel
with one shot."

Side by side, the bodies lie on the lawn.
Three magpies are leaping around them.
Already they have ripped out the guts
and pecked out the eyes.
As we chat about roses,
flies are crawling through the fur
and feasting in the sockets.
By dawn,
after a night of badgers and foxes,
the lawn will be tidy again,
spotless and smooth
under the roses.

COUNTRY LIFE

One evening in early May,
my farmer neighbour, Ron,
widower, eighty-one,
knocks at my door.
Locked himself out.
Lost his keys.
Could he phone, please?

He phones a daughter,
leaves a message.
We drink mugs of tea,
we sit, we chat and we wait.
The phone stays silent.

Then we go into his garden,
search everywhere he's been.
Sheds, greenhouses,
flowerbeds and vegetables,
all neat, tidy and perfect.
His daughter's empty stable,
his son's abandoned aviary,
the paddock and the hen run,
clucking with hens,
the cockerel crowing.
A lifetime,
laid out and orderly,
on the ground, and in the soil,
everywhere he's been.

We search, almost inch by inch,
running fingers through the grasses,
bluebells and primroses.
Then, Ron remembers . . .
Children's birthday party,
somewhere . . .
after piano lessons,
somewhere . . .
She could be hours more,
Husband up in London,
somewhere . . .

I remind myself I have to go.
I've booked to see the village play.
The evening is warm,
he won't die of cold.
Ron hates the indoor life.
He is an outdoor man.
I go with my conscience clear.
Absurd Person Singular.
I leave Ron, alone in his acres,
amid the lengthening shadows,
waiting.
Singular, but not absurd,
just a widower,
eighty-one years old.

FOX

On the way through the woods
this morning,
I saw a young fox
sitting in the middle of the path,
a silhouette,
as still as stone.

We stopped and stared,
the dog on the lead,
taut as an arrow in the bow,
pointing.
We all three stood still,
staring and silent.

Butterflies flickered
in the sun's rays,
slanting through the trees.
A distant plane was heard,
high above.
Minutes passed.

The dog lost interest
and turned its head away.
Somewhere in the woods,
an animal coughed.
The fox, the dog and I
stayed still.

It was so young,
perhaps I was the first human
it had seen.
Aloof and indifferent,
as foxes always are,
what did it make of me?

Not much, it seems.
Unhurried, it stood up,
turned away
and silently disappeared
into the nettles.

Not much
to write home about.

PRODNOSE: What's that got to do with
old age and death?

Nothing.

PRODNOSE: So what's it in for then?

I like it.

PRODNOSE: Now you're just rambling.
That *is* old age.
You're forgiven.

THE HERON

Silent, effortless,
as the sun sets,
the heron flaps over the treetops.
Awkward as a learner,
sharp as a dart.
Yellow stalk legs lower,
dangle with ungainly elegance.
Grey wings fold shut like a book.
A microlight crawls across the sky,
on a line of noise.
The angler reels in his line,
unhooks his fly,
takes off his spectacles
and packs up his tackle.
A better fisher has come.
As the sun sets,
the heron stares over her lake,
at the top of the tree,
as still as stone.

TIME PASSING

Late afternoon,
in the water meadow,
the wind behind us,
blowing the sound away,
the train rushes past,
half hidden by the hedge,
silver and silent
as a ghost in the sun.

A face glances out,
sees me, sees Jess,
wonders, perhaps,
who we are
and where they are,
in a different time,
a different space.
A passing of ghosts.

NOISY NEIGHBOUR

One afternoon
upstairs
reading, dozing
BONK THUD RUMBLE
uh . . . noisy neighbours
BONK RUMBLE THUD
wake up
detached house
no neighbours
forgot
what then?
BONK BONK
burglars?
creep downstairs
look
nothing
BONK RUMBLE BONK
side wall
listen
look out window
wood pile
RUMBLE BONK
back door
go round
up on roof
over woodpile
peer down

RUMBLE RUMBLE
suddenly
badger
big one
hairless back
bare bum
mange
poor beast

no doctor
no nurse
nothing
just get on with it
RUMBLE BONK
just get on
with it
RUMBLE RUMBLE
BONK
just
get
on
with
it

life

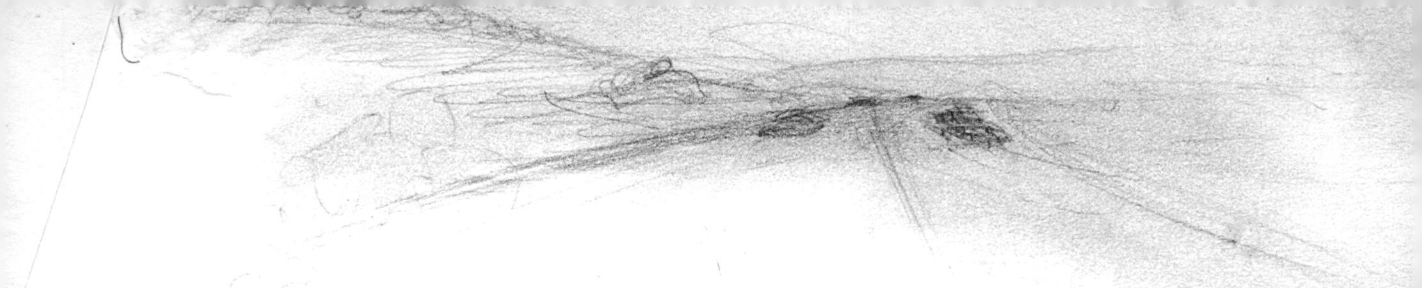

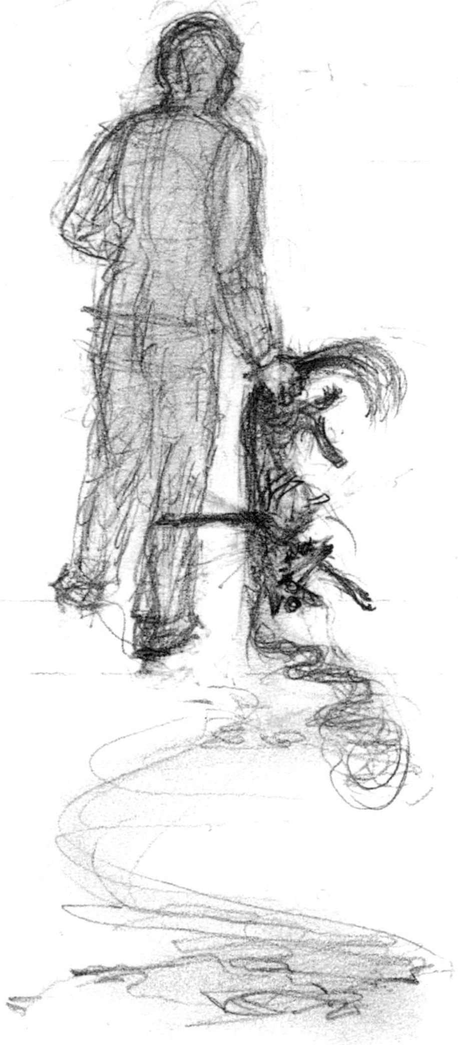

DEATH ON THE ROAD

Ahead,
in the middle of the road,
a bundle of fur.
I drive past a smashed fox,
signal a right,
swerve across and park.
Cars hoot as they scream past.
Ten seconds in the car,
walking back seems minutes.
Cars thrash by, buffeting wind and tyres.
Then, at last, a space.
All is quiet and still.
For a few seconds, it is safe.

I pick up the fox,
unsticking it from the blackening blood,
leaving bits of guts stuck to the tarmac,
carry it to the hedge
and lay it amongst leaves.
Its stomach bashed open,
intestines trailing,
teeth choked with blood,
one leg at an angle, like a stick,
an eye dangling.
I pick up handfuls of dried grass
and cover her.
Futile, but better than the road.

As I turn away,
the flies are gathering.

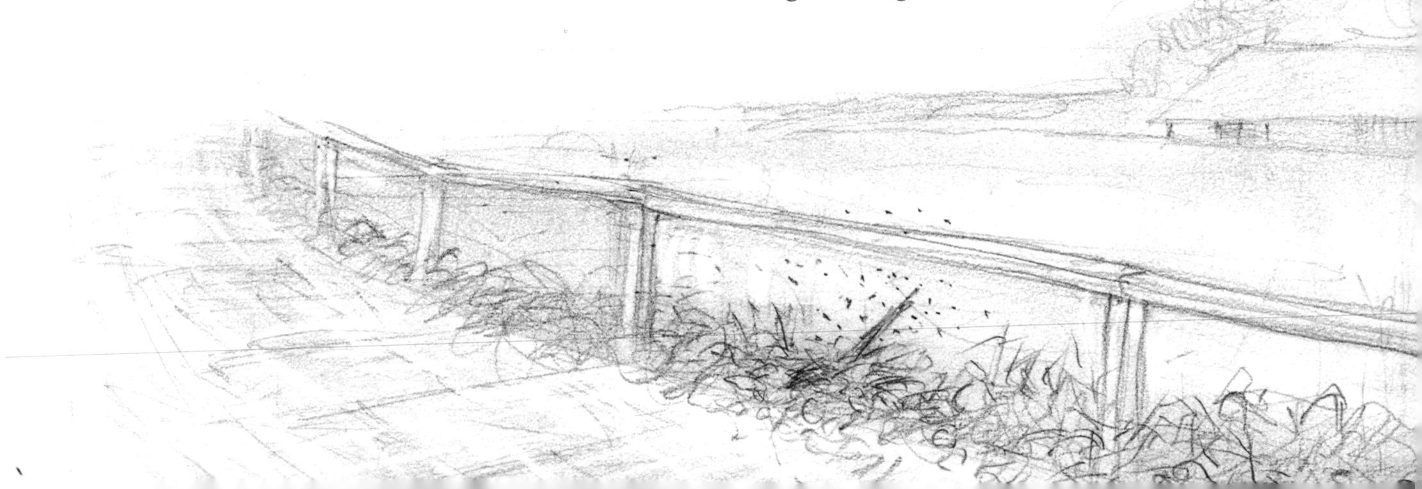

As the years go by, it slowly dawns on you . . . go to a business meeting, go to a party, you are always the oldest person in the room.

The people you work for and who boss you about are young enough to be your children. They tell you what to do and how to do it, and you were doing it *decades* before they were born. Even more galling is that they are often right. More in touch, more up to date. Bum.

But they are all twerps just the same. (Now, *there's* an old-fashioned word. Does anyone under sixty say "twerp"?)

PRODNOSE: 'Course they don't, dumbo'

You gradually realise there is no older generation ahead of you: you are on your own.

Apart from one or two unusual people in their eighties and nineties, most people in your life have died, often long ago.

You are in the vanguard,* your turn next to enter the tunnel.

It's difficult to realise.

* Not the Guard's van. They were in the back, and have been done away with. More's the pity.

PRODNOSE you left loads of empty space!

Shut up, Prodnose
It's called Design

BUSINESS LUNCH

A business lunch meant going somewhere you would rather not go to meet people to meet people you would rather not meet to eat food and drink drink you will later regret to make plans that more often than not come to nought and spend money that could better be spent

How was it?

Oh, OK
Goddam Business lunches all the same.

Went to the office first.

Room after room of female teenagers staring at screens.

No one doing any work.

No one talking

No one with a pen or pencil in their hand.

Half dead.

I couldn't draw it.
Too deadly dull.

It was like a mausoleum —

Completely silent, the house of the living dead.

They might as well have been in coffins, trying to communicate with people in other graves.

Oh, Come on —

No!
They even E-mail someone they can see across the room!

Too legless. to walk over and talk to them.

Then, tucked away in the corner, was this old bloke –

grey-haired, balding – must have been at least fifty.

Twenty years younger than you.

Shut up! But he was a freak.

He was actually on his feet moving about...

just like a human being, really weird. Probably a cleaner.

Even the senior people, all girlies, of course, have only just turned thirty

Where are all the old people? People with maturity and experience?

PRODNOSE: Shall I tell you?

No! Bog off, Prodnose.

You know my teen-aged Children's Editor?

Met her mother today. Up in town for her SIXTIETH BIRTHDAY!

Not only is my editor much younger than me –

her mother is ELEVEN YEARS younger than me!

Then, last week, when I did that radio programme,

Chatting to the producer afterwards, a girlie, of course –

I said, Blimey! Just realised I was last on this programme 27 years ago – 1977.

"Oh?" She said. "1977? That's the year I was born."

TOTAL COLLAPSE OF ELDERLY PARTY

It's insane. I think I'll die now.

Oh, no. Got to go out tonight. Jazz club.

Would be tonight – just when I wanted to die.

PRODNOSE:
What about the pictures for this page? Where are they?

No room.

No energy more like!
T.A.T.T.
Tired All The Time?

NO!

Bad design then.

Look, it's the same two people in the same room. Why keep drawing them every time they speak?
BORING! POINTLESS!

Posy Simmonds can do it.

Yeah, yeah, well . . .
She's just a youngster.
She'll learn.

JAZZ CLUB

local pub
jazz club
arrive early
almost empty
front rows
four pairs
white heads

old ladies
in here?
but why?
W.I.?

soon depart
when jazz
starts!
their poor
old hearts

but
when jazz
blasts out
eight white heads
start bobbing about!

what's this?
aged geriatric
jazz fans?
lady OAPs
jazz devotees?

but
come to think of it
they must be
almost
as old
as
me

10.45 pm. *BEDTIME*

Oh, my God, here we go again
Let the Old Age Rigmarole begin.

STAGE ONE:
Tidy sitting room. Sort newspapers.

Keep *Radio Times*. Keep *Times2* for crossword.

Chuck papers back hallway. Bin tomorrow.

Roll pouffe over to bookcase.

Pick up dog blanket.

Remember pick up TV glasses, put in case.

Take wine glass to kitchen.

Switch off telly, unplug. Switch off heater,
unplug.

Unplug aerial or death by lightning.
ANXIETY.
(House opposite struck, watching TV in
thunderstorm.)

Put on main light. Switch off side lights.

Pick up notebook, pencil. Check glasses
round neck, not lost in sofa.

Missus tidies sofa, plumps cushions, adjusts
covers, etc. (all old ladies do it, my mum did.
I wouldn't bother.)

Take special back cushion upstairs.

Both do all this.

> DONE! 14 minutes 37 seconds.

A trouble shared
is a trouble halved.   PRODNOSE: Don't you
                                 believe it.

                        For once I agree.

STAGE TWO

Kitchen. Play Lester Young CD, keep spirits up   in the face of adversity.

Clean worktops, cooker top and table. Stack.

Run hot water (no dishwasher – too complicated,modern, difficult, tiresome, boring.)

Wash up. Leave to drain and dry.

Put on kettle for hot water bottle and two mugs warm water . . . (latest Old Age craze – *warm* water.)

Set out tray, two mugs cold, two mugs warm.

Rinse bowl, sink. Dry up. (I wouldn't bother, but . . .)

Put china, cutlery away. Drying-up cloth on radiator.

DONE! 17 minutes 22 seconds.

TOTAL so far: 31 minutes 59 seconds.

STAGE THREE

Bedroom. Bathroom.

Clean teeth, etc. Take dog out garden.

Take up tray of mugs. Put out main light.

Put down tray. Switch on bedside lights.
Switch off main light.
Forgot dog blanket.
Go down get dog blanket.

Turn down bed. Arrange pillows for sitting.
Go down, get bag.
Get other bag, containing current work (this) . . .

DONE! 12 minutes 21 seconds.

TOTAL: 43 minutes 20 seconds.

Check my bedside equipment.
1. Tissues
2. Handkerchief
3. Torch
4. Pills
5. Eyeshades
6. Pencils
7. Notebook
8. Glasses
9. Two mugs water
10. Books

ORL PRESENT AND KORRECT, SAH!

AT LAST! GET INTO BED! SUCCESS!

R . . . E . . . L . . . A . . . X . . .

Get up, go down for pee.

PRODNOSE: You really are
an old fuddy-duddy.

Tell me something
I don't know, Prodnose.
Good bogging night.

Hmmm . . .
Better see if they're still in business . . .
Only 3/9d. inc. Tax.

'lease write for illust
Folder and name
nearest stockist.

PIFCO, LTD.
Manchester, 4.

10x 14'11

BUNIONS!
THE CAUSE REACHED AND REMOVED

Some years ago, a clever French chemist perfected a Balm, the unique penetrative power of which enabled it to reach the root-cause of the bunion, to relieve the pain and to attack the distressing condition at its source. This Balm has been widely sold on the Continent as B.D. Baume Dalet for many years, and it is now available in this country. After two or three applica-tions, the agonising pain is subdued, the inflammation reduced. Gradually the hard growth between the joints is softened, dissolved and dispersed, and the big toe is naturally enabled to re-gain its healthy size and position. B.D. Baume Dalet does more, than give relief from pain; it acts directly on the cause, with the promise of permanent improvement. Give B.D. Baume Dalet an early trial. From all chemists 3/9d. inc. Tax. In case of difficulty, post free 4/-, from the sole Distributors: Wilsons Chemical Products Ltd., (Dept. 232), 18, Old Town, London, S.W.4.

THE RATIONALIST

I don't believe in "auras",
Or the "spirit of the place",
It's all nonsense, of course.

Nevertheless,
Up on the hill, near the church,
There is always a feeling of peace.
You could almost say,
an aura of peace.

High above, the planes fly over,
Distant traffic is heard,
But there seems to be a stillness,
A silence,
Which feels eternal.

It's all nonsense, of course.

I don't believe in the "spirit of the place".
Nor do I believe in "auras".
Nevertheless,
Up on the hill, near the church,
There is one.

Dammit.

NIGHT THOUGHTS

Thank God, or Someone,
I am not in pain.
As far as I know,
I am in good health.
There is no war.
Tonight, no bombers will come.
Tomorrow will bring no invader.
We are at peace.

The bed is comfortable.
I am warm.
The rain will fall on the roof,
Not on me.
The cold ground is far below.
The wind blows, the curtain stirs,
I do not feel it.
If frost comes, it will be outside.

Inside, the room is warm.
I am not hungry.
I am not thirsty.
There is no famine.
There is no drought.

I am not alone,
I can hear breathing.
I can see.
I can hear.
I can walk.
And I can sleep.

One day, one night,
Death will come,
but not just yet.
For the time being,
All is well.

Being over seventy is like being engaged in a war.
All our friends are going or gone and we survive
among the dead and the dying as on a battlefield.

MURIEL SPARK
Memento Mori

LIFE ON THE BATTLEFIELD
Christmas is such a happy family time.

Survivors of seventy or more are in a very vulnerable
position. The spectre of loneliness stalks the empty
spaces of the battlefield.

If you have no children, you have no
grandchildren. Other members of your family –
mother, father, aunts, uncles – are long dead. There is
no generation ahead of you and no generation behind
you. You may have no brothers or sisters, or if you
have, they are often far away or dead. There may be a
few cousins, but cousins are rarely close and often
barely keep in touch.

At "family" times such as Christmas the survivors
may find themselves quite alone, without a partner or
a family and dependent upon friends. But most
friends do have families and over Christmas their
houses are packed with grown-up sons, daughters and
grandchildren.

These survivors may have to retreat to their
dugouts and wait for the "festive season" to blow
over.

MEMENTO MORI

If I had my life over again
I should form the habit
of nightly composing myself
to thoughts of death.
I would practise, as it were,
the remembrance of death.
There is no other practice
which so intensifies life.

THEN

When you get old, you tend to think back on
your early life, not middle age, but childhood;
your parents and how you came to be . . . don't
you think?

As you're now coming to the end, I suppose it is
natural to think of the beginning.

PRODNOSE: *You're always going on about
the past. And childhood. You've made a
profession out of it.*

> You haven't got a profession, Prodnose.
> Except being a bore. Yes! That's it!
> You're a professional bore.

So I have *got a profession, then?*

> Bore off, Prodnose.

Even the most trivial things remind you of Mum
and Dad and the passing of time. Seeing that
cardboard box outside the junk shop – BOOKS £1
. . . 1895 . . . So incredibly long ago! One hundred
and ten years. It seems impossible that I knew
someone who was alive then. It's so remote it
seems like life on a different planet.

BOOKS £1

Royal Academy Pictures
1895
The year my mother was born.
What a world for Mum to come into!

It was mostly posh ladies
gazing haughtily,
or hairy old men,
with beards and moustaches,
glaring grimly.

Poor Mum.

All around were miles and miles
of rural landscape.
Miles of it,
filled with rural animals
and sunsets.
In 1895,
the sun was setting all the time.

There were no men
in 1895,
apart from the hairy old men
with beards and moustaches.
All the men were down at the seaside,
being fishermen.
How would Mum ever get married,
in Sydenham?

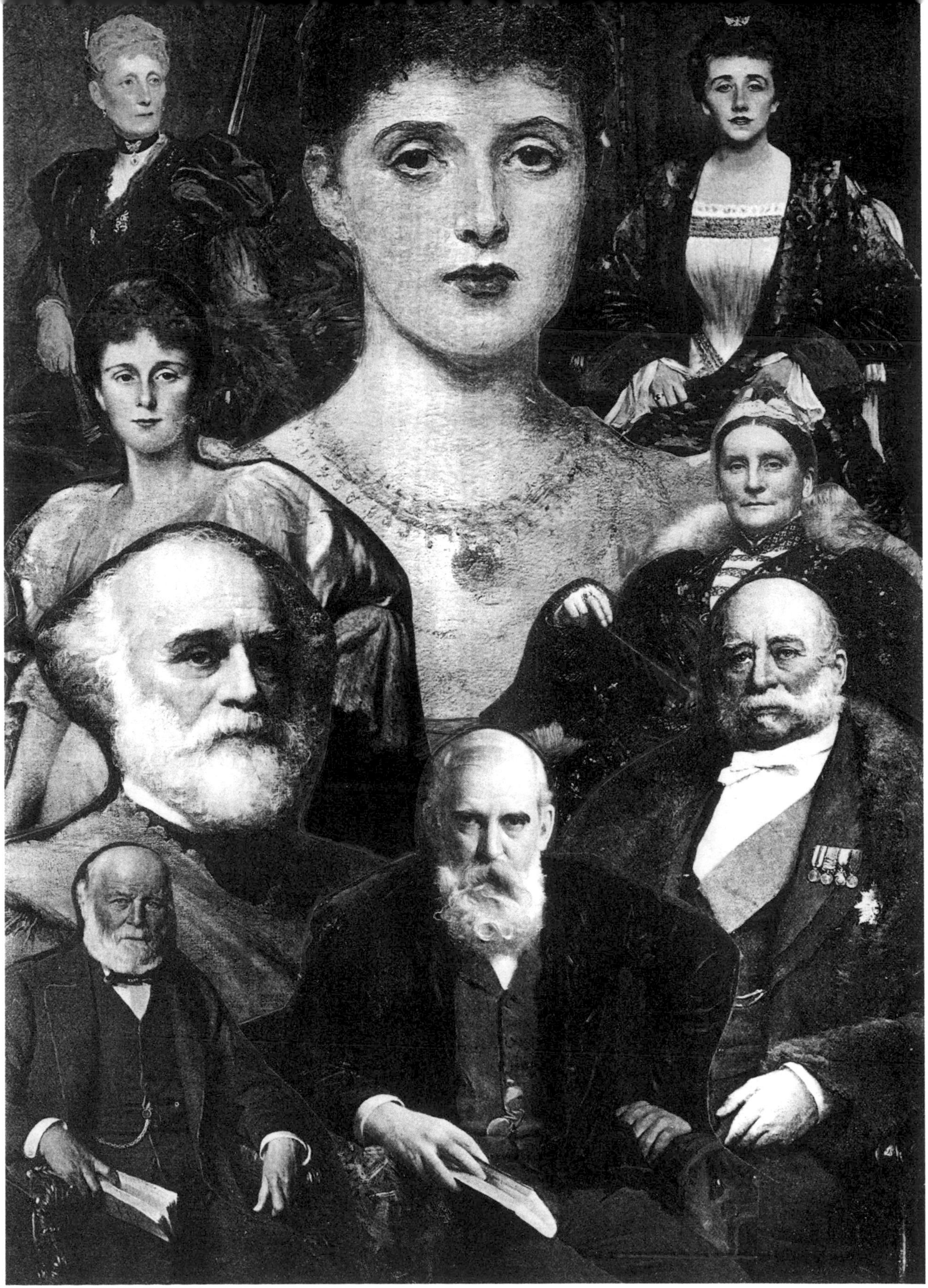

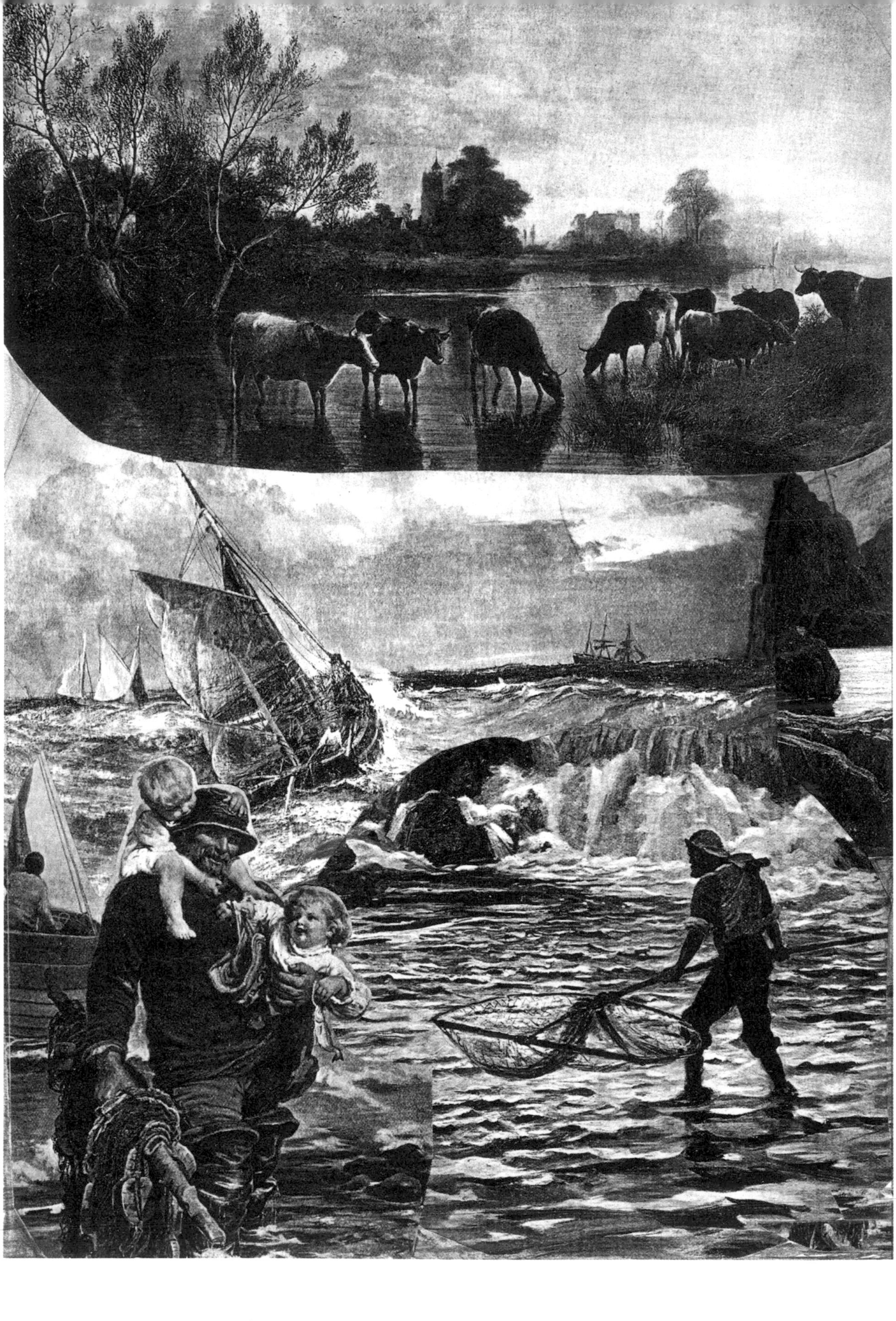

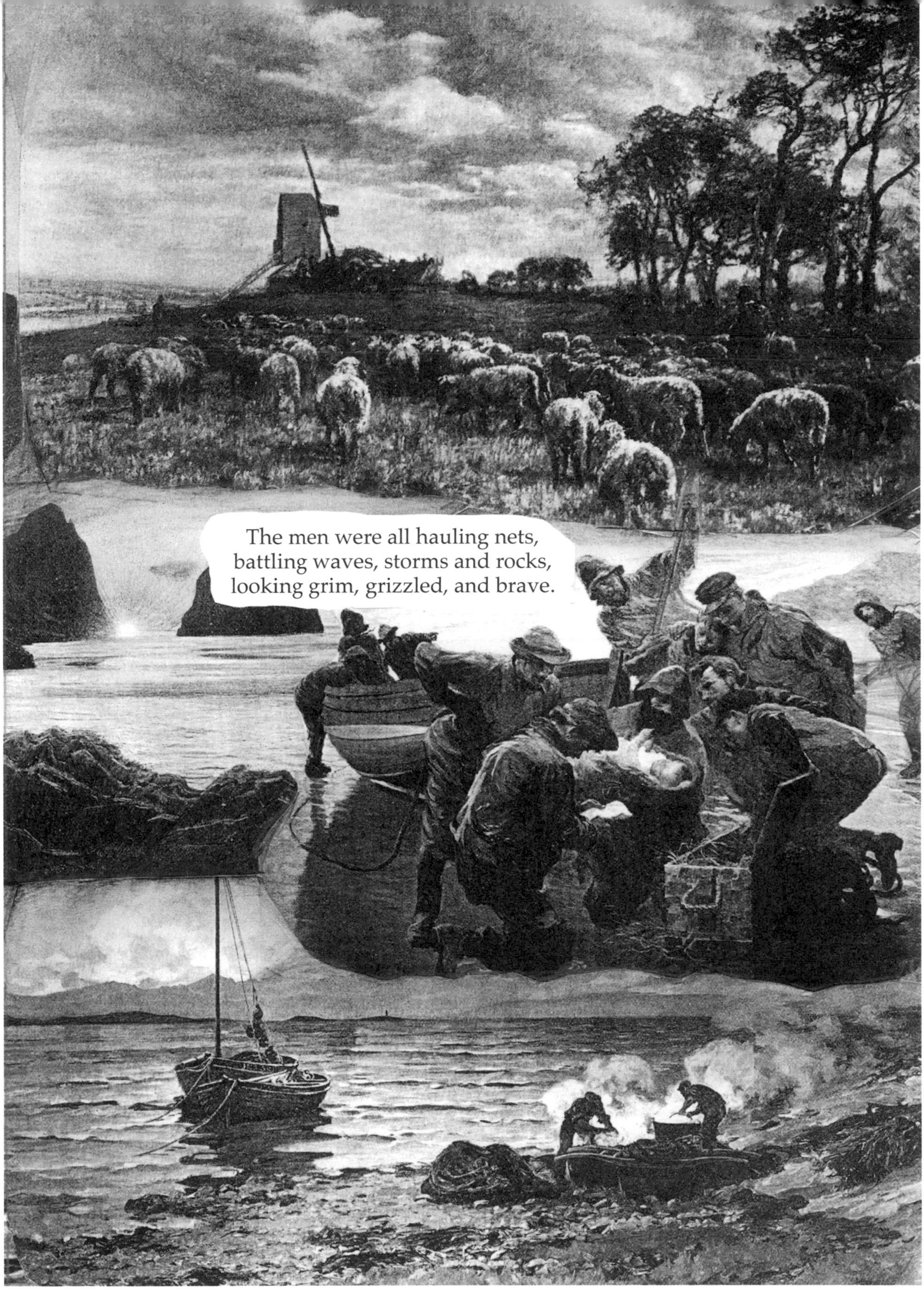
The men were all hauling nets,
battling waves, storms and rocks,
looking grim, grizzled, and brave.

But then, in 1895, most of the people were little girls.
There were no little boys for Mum to fall in love with.
There were little girls with flowers, little girls with
kittens, little girls with puppies.

In 1895, most of the little girls
were asleep. Aah!
Lots more were dying.
They were dying all over the place,
usually beside the cottage fire,
in a wooden chair, with a pillow
at their back. Aah!

Glad Mum didn't die as a little girl.

And the poor! Oh, the poor poor!
In 1895 everyone was poor, except for the posh
ladies and the hairy old men.
The poor stood nobly at their cottage gates, or
struggled bravely with their fishing boats, or
fiddled with their fish.

In 1895, the poor looked so nice
in their cosy-shabby clothes.
Mum would have felt at home
with the poor. Except for the fish.

My dad was very lucky, born at just the right time. Death was hovering over the young boys of his generation, already filling in his order book and planning his diary.

Death feeds us up, keeps an eye on our weight, and herds us like pigs through the abbatoir gate.

PALLADAS (4th–5th century)
The Greek Anthology
(trans Tony Harrison)

The affection of a father
and a son are different:
the father loves the person
of the son, and the son loves
the memory of his father.

ANON

MY DAD AND THE HISTORY OF THE TWENTIETH CENTURY

Even before he was born,
my dad,
swimming about in the waters,
knew exactly when to get out.

Born,
5 November 1900

Fourteen,
5 November 1914.
Too young.

Eighteen,
5 November 1918.
Just ripe for slaughter.

Six days later,
11 November 1918,
War ends.

Armistice.

Phew!
Just missed it.

1939,
Here we go again.
Thirty-nine now,
Too old.

Phew!
Just missed it again.

Well done, Dad.
You deserve a medal,
for life saving.

DAD AND ME

Seventy-one.
By now
Dad was dead.

Died
Two months before
Seventy-one.

I had cancer.
He had cancer.

Mine was cut out.
His wasn't.

He died.
I didn't.

So far.
So good.

For me.

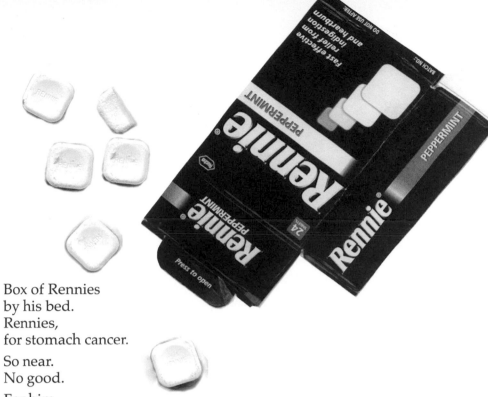

Box of Rennies
by his bed.
Rennies,
for stomach cancer.

So near.
No good.

For him.

85

PRODNOSE:
I think you're a bit
obsessed with your
parents.

Yes, well –
getting born is just
as random and
accidental as dying.

LOVE

1930

Ethel
housemaid
dusting

Ernest
milkman
cycling

Ethel
duster
shaking

Ernest
passing

waves

1934
me

DAD

Away on holiday,
when I phone the hospital.
they say:
"Your father is dying."

As I try to run
to the car, I hear
a passing woman say:
"Has that man got hay fever?"

Hoping to be in time
we drive to the hospital,
and find him sitting up,
so we have a chat.

We stay the night
in his empty house
and lie awake, remembering
the fear we had seen in his eyes.

Next day,
when I go in,
he is sitting on the bed,
swinging his legs.

Luckily,
he has his back to me,
or he would see
my disappointment.

I think: Bloody hell, Dad,
if you're going to die,
for God's sake,
get on with it.

Don't sit swinging your legs
like a little boy.
Get on with it,
and die.

Then, later,
in the middle of the night,
they phone.
He has got on with it.

Next morning,
when I go in to pick up
the usual black bin bag –
pyjamas, pants, vest, etcetera

A young nurse says:
"He was such a dear old man."

AUNTIES

When I was a child,
There were always lots of
aunties.
They were everywhere.

Some were real aunties –
Mum's umpteen sisters,
Dad's umpteen sisters.
There was no end of them.

Auntie Flo, Auntie Betty,
Auntie Edie, Auntie Marjorie,
Auntie Bertha, Auntie Jessie . . .
The list is endless.

I won't go on,
Except for Auntie Violet,
My favourite Auntie,
killed on a bus in the Blitz.

It seemed quite natural,
Didn't give it a thought.
That was the way the world was –
Lots of old ladies everywhere.

They were called spinsters.
Some were rather quaint
And looked down upon.
A few were slightly mad.

Then, one day,
When I was grown up,
It dawned on me –

First World War

A million men were missing.
Why hadn't I thought of it before?
The men these women never met,
Never even had the chance to
meet.

All dead.

These ladies were always kind,
Gentle and loving to me.
Not sour, bitter and resentful,
As they had every right to be.

A million missing men.
A million aunties.

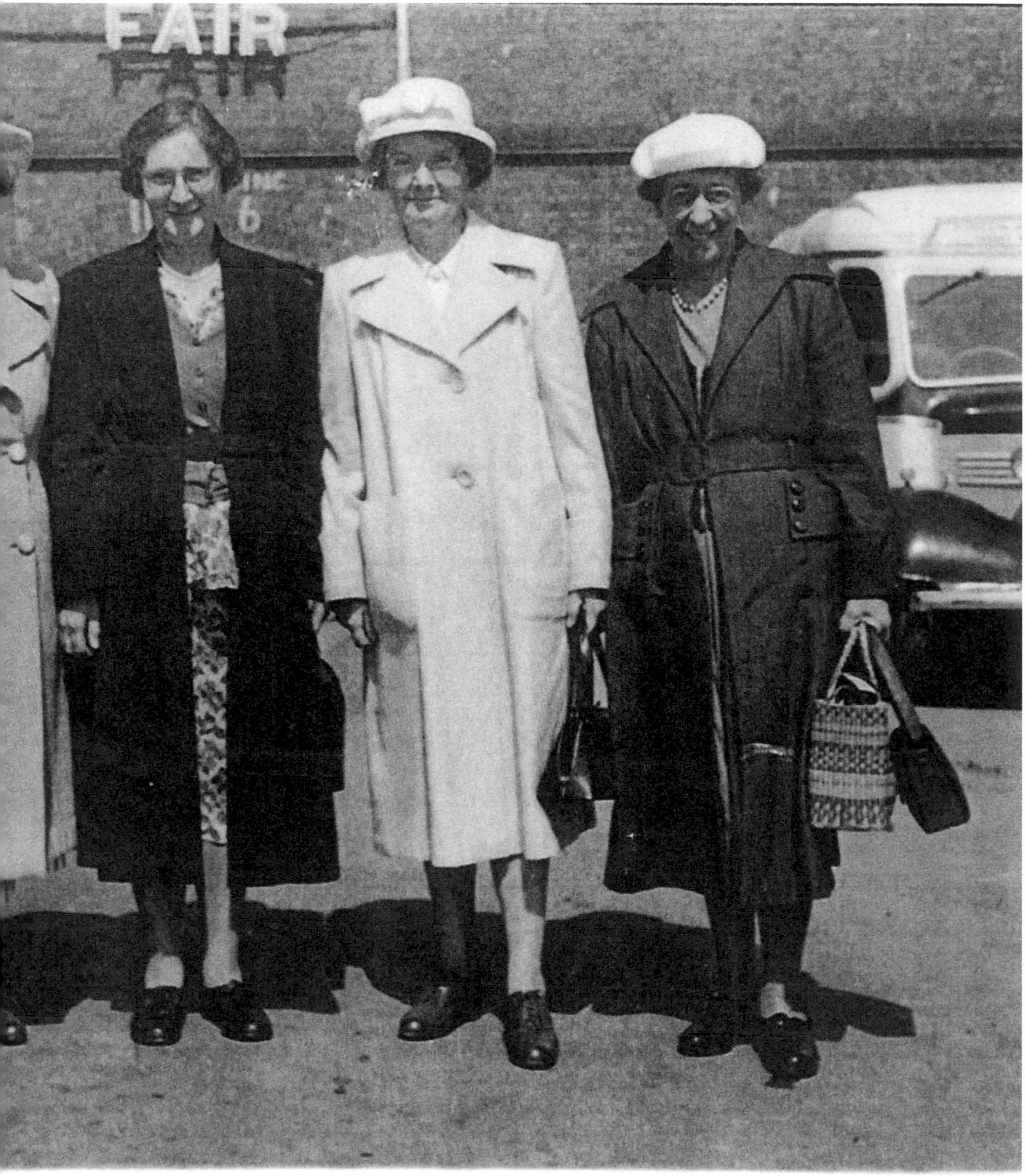
FAIR

Two of the spinster aunties looked
after me in the Second World War,
when Death was everywhere.

EVACUATED 1941

Auntie Betty, Auntie Flo,
my teddy bear and me
all asleep in Betty's cottage.
No air raid sirens now,
no A.R.P.,
here in deepest Dorset,
far from London
bombs and blitz.

Sudden roar
of aircraft engines,
very loud and very low.
The little windows rattled,
the cottage seemed to shake.
Then a different louder rattle,
very loud and very near,
Machine gun fire.

Out of bed,
hearts thumping –
"Get the cases, Flo!"
(Three cases, always at the ready,
packed and waiting,
ready for Invasion
and escape.)
Down the curved stone stairs we go.

Standing, trembling,
By the dying fire,
Crying, waiting . . .
What to do?
Where to go?
With our cases,
In our dressing gowns,
Through the winter night.

Auntie, where is Jerry now?
Are they coming, Auntie Betty?
Are they here already?
Will they kill us, Auntie Flo?
Was it one of ours?
If they missed,
Where did the bullets go?

Is it the Invasion, Auntie?
No, just a dogfight,
I suppose, dear.
What dogs, Auntie?
Jerry dogs and ours?
Now, don't you worry, boy.
Better you get back to bed.
Go on, up you go.

Up stone steps to bed,
to twist and turn
and lie and dream
of bullets, bombs,
big dogs and guns
and Germans
bashing down our door.

Aunties and War and
fear were a big part of
childhood.

And of course, there
was also the
the mind-broadening
long distance travel.

GEOGRAPHY

One day
In the Infants Class
at the village school,
in Stour Provost,
Dorset,
Miss Dominic said:
"This country is an island."

How could it be
an ISLAND?
I had travelled
HOURS and HOURS
in the charabanc,
HOURS and HOURS
all the way from
Wimbledon Park!

We even had to stop
halfway for a wee.
Auntie Flo bought me
a choc ice.
Walls. Fourpence.
Auntie Flo had a tuppeny cornet.
Walls. Tuppence.
I like Lyons ices best.

I had travelled
ONE HUNDRED AND TEN MILES!
All on my own,
(with Auntie Flo).
The longest journey in
all my life.
Now Miss says it was
all on an ISLAND!

Even the seaside was
HOURS and HOURS
away in the charabanc.
I had been there, too
so I knew.
(It is at a place called Weymouth.)

(THINKS)
Islands are little round
things with a tree
in the middle.
The sea is all around
with sharks in.
That's an island,
Miss.

(THINKS)

If this gigantic great
lump of land
is an ISLAND,
Please Miss,
WHERE ARE THE EDGES?

Even whilst still a student, you begin
to realise the odd nature of time.
Its different speeds at different ages.

TIME AND MISS APPLEBY

"Miss Appleby?
Oh yes, she's still there,
still with the Infants."

"Oh no, she can't be,
she taught *me*!
Donkey's years ago."

Dammit.
I was grown up,
a painter,
(painting naked women)
motorbike,
girlfriend,
ex-Army.
Miss Appleby taught me
before the War!

"Before the War"
was a different era –
ancient,
prehistoric,
lost in the blitz
of time.

Dear old Miss Appleby,
silver-haired and apple-cheeked,
(she had the right name)
we all loved her.
You wanted to cuddle her.
She was like a mum.

But she was *old*.
Old *then*.
By now she must be . . .
              about a hundred.
                    Or dead.

I had been years in Elementary School.
              years in Dorset evacuated.
              years in bugger rugger Grammar School,
              years in Catterick eternity Army.
              years in Art School.
                    (painting naked women).

"No, she's still there.
Lovely woman.
All the children love her.
Still lives in the same house.
Retiring soon.
We'll all miss her."

Miss Appleby,
still in the same school?
              in the same class?
              in the same house?
still *alive*?
              after all that time?

A lifetime.

A lifetime
Of fifteen years.

SIX YEARS

June 2007.
Today,
in the kitchen,
turned out a drawer.
Scottish Oatcakes,
five packets.
BEST BEFORE:
JAN. 2001.
Six years.
What happened to that time?
Nothing much.
Can't remember . . .
It just . . .
Passed away.

June 1945.
My father-in-law,
home again.
Fought in the desert,
North Africa,
Italy, Monte Cassino,
etcetera.
Military Medal.
Demob, home, wife,
bus to the office.
What happened in that time?
Nothing much.
There was just . . .
a War.

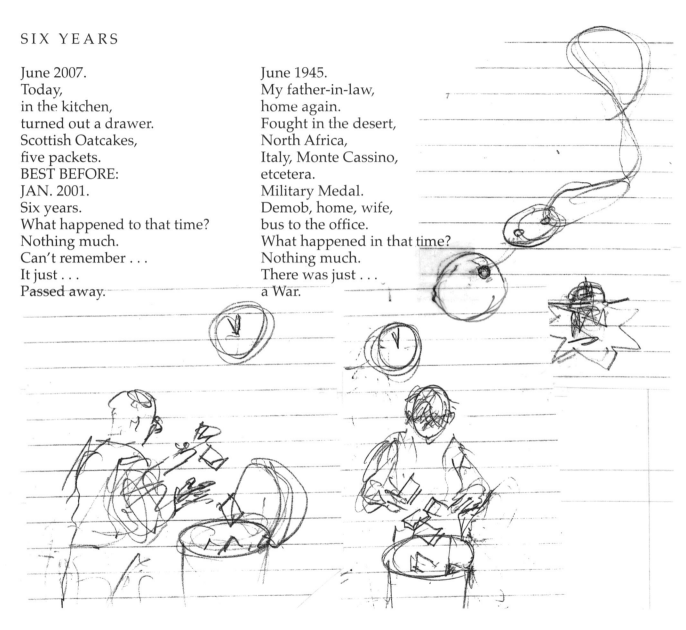

Even when young, you are constantly made aware of the passing of
time. You are always older than you think you are.

THE MIRROR

After thirty-four years,
the old mirror from home,
clumsy and ugly,
not even quaint or kitsch,
is still in my garage.
I can't throw it away,
I can't have it in the house,
it just doesn't fit anywhere.
It has been there since
Mum and Dad died.

All my life,
it hung over the kitchen fireplace.

Dad kept his Mentholatum
on the ledge behind it,
antidote to London smogs.
My Radio Malt,
its blue and yellow label
with the blazing sun,
was kept warm there.
For years,
I measured my height in it,
judging my head against
the reflected window frame.

Was I ever going to grow?

Now its silver is blotched,
its shelves broken off,
it lies in three dusty pieces.
Dad bought it
from a costermonger,
on his milk round
and walked it home
on the pedal of his bike,
long before the war.
He said it cost
"half a dollar".

How can I throw it away?
I must repair it
and hang it,
if only in the garage.
It's been with me now
for seventy years.
I'll definitely repair it,
one day,
soon,
when there is time.

GETTING SENTIMENTAL

The breadboard I use today,
and the knife,
have been with me
all my life.

Mum and Dad were using them
before the War.
They all survived
the doodlebugs and Blitz.

After all,
it takes a lot to blow
a breadboard and a knife
to bits.

And it takes a lot from life,
to not get sentimental
about a breadboard
and a knife.

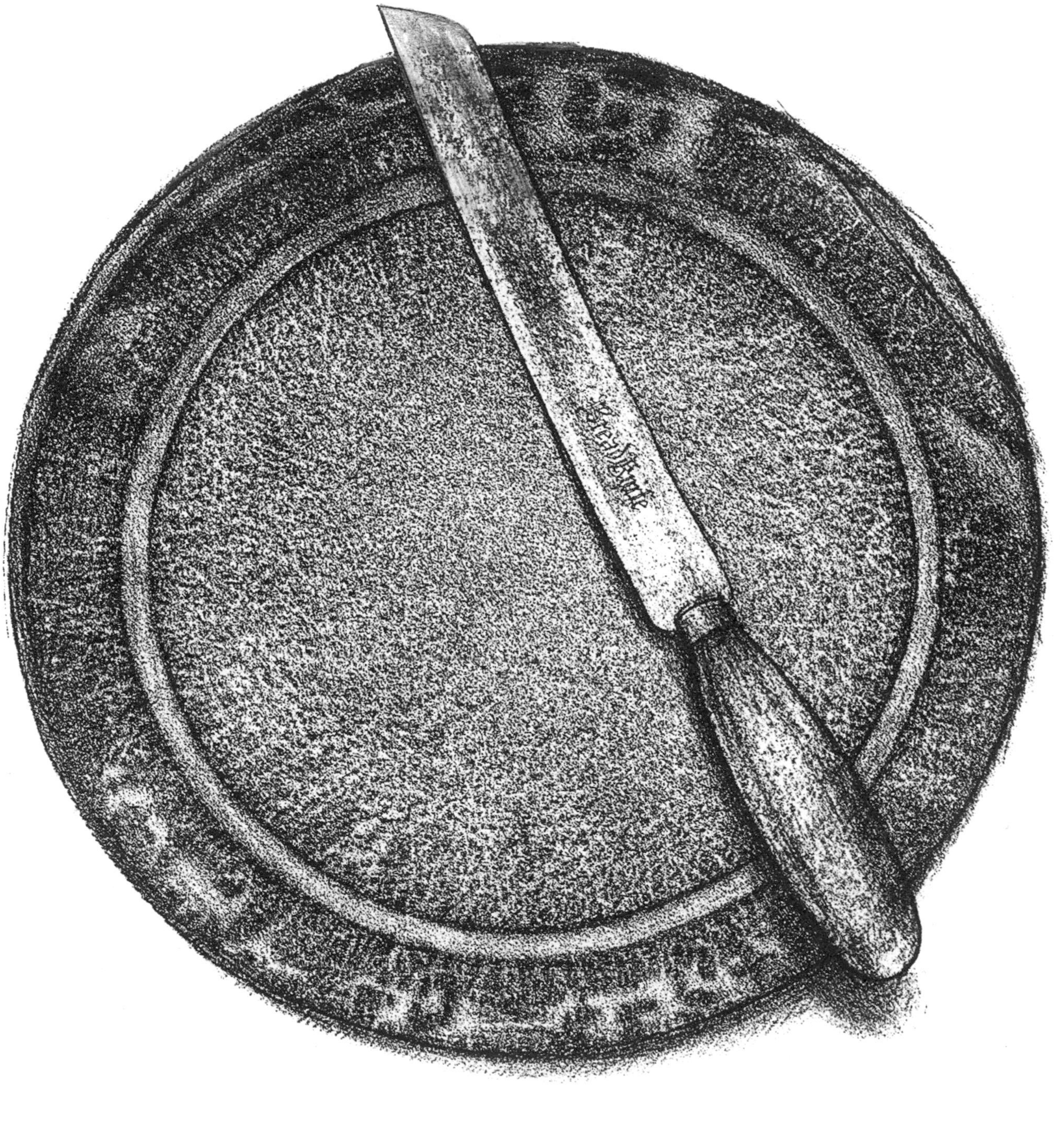

1945

War ended,
Bombed houses,
Mike, Tom and me
Soldiers,
Scrambling, fighting, climbing
Stacks of slates.

Scream

Mike's shoe slipped
Between slate stacks'
Jagged edges
Leg dragged out

Scream

Gash blood leg red
Deep
Blood-soaked sock
Blood
Shiny wet on shoe
Sock black with blood
Mike white

Mummy Mummy Mummy
Running down our street
Mummy Mummy Mummy

Tom and me,
Numb, dumb,
Follow
Drops on path,
Smears on step.

Mike gone in.
Door closed.
No more soldiers.
War ended.

Not every bombed house meant that
someone had been killed, but nevertheless
they should have been a reminder of death.

   To us, they were just playgrounds. We
could do as much damage as we liked, with
never a thought about what might have
happened there.

RITCHIE

We were outside my house
running round Ritchie
four or five of us
clutching the ends
of his school scarf
round and round
we ran
yelling laughing
Ritchie grinning
spinning round and round
laughing

Till the knot   neck flesh bulges
got tight   over rope
we saw his face   Ritchie's eyes bulge
crimson   stare
turning purple   tongue sticks up
his lips   lips spittle
going blue
                        fingers weak
quick quick   scrabbling
                        whimpering

panicky fingers
digging
at rope of wool   then   we all stand
buried   somehow   trembling
in reddening neck   at last . . .   one of us in tears
wool hard as wood   the scarf comes free someone helps Ritchie up
tight   no one says sorry
                        Ritchie drops   we all wander off
                        kneels
                        gasping   I go indoors
quick quick   shoulders heaving   for tea

Very soon after the war Death struck nearby,
closer than the corner shop. Three boys who lived
only yards fom me were killed on the road.

IVOR BRIDGES   11   Braemar Avenue
ALFRED HAINES   16   Normanton Avenue
ALAN BAKER   13   Mount Road

It seemed to be random, just bad luck.
It won't happen to me . . .

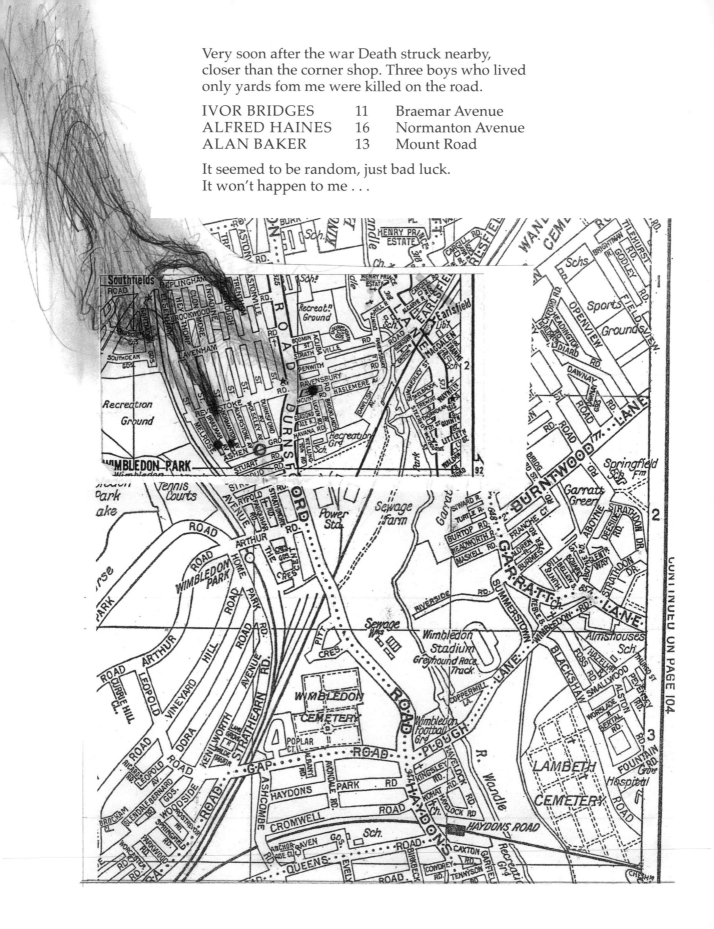

BOMBS GONE

In the war,
every night,
Londoners went down
into the Underground,
hoping to escape the bombs
exploded by young men
from Germany,
sitting high in the sky above.

Today,
every day,
Londoners go down
into the Underground,
hoping to escape the bombs
exploded by young men
from Yorkshire,
sitting deep in the ground below.

In those olden days
war was so simple.
You fought it,
you won it,
and when it ended,
you put out flags
and gave a party.
Then, there was peace.

Bombs gone.
It was all so simple.

GYP

Took Gyp to the vet
to be put down.
Dear, neurotic old Gyp,
badly treated when young.
Frightened of boots
and men in hats.
Bit of a snob,
didn't like the working class.
Barked at them.
Liked to bite them.
Getting her own back.

Standing on the vet's table,
waiting for the injection,
she looks into my eyes,
trusting . . .
Stroking her head,
stroking . . .
Suddenly, she slumps.
"That's it," says the vet.
"No heart action now."

Then they took her away
to burn.

The randomness of death is
the worst thing about it. Who
is "chosen" to live and who to
die. If you don't believe in a
god, then there is no choosing.
Nevertheless, the arbitrariness
of living or dying seems, if not
the choice of a god, to be the
fall of dice thrown by a blind
gambler. Or in wartime, the
movement of someone's foot.

BOMBER 1944

An insurance clerk
of twenty-two
now a bomber pilot
became fixated
by his foot

He found that if
he tensed his foot
slightly
during the final bomb run
the rudder would move
slightly
and the bomber would drift
slightly
to the left or to the right
so slightly
even his bomb aimer
would be unaware

Bombs gone!

A ton of bombs
then fell
on slightly different streets
on slightly different houses
and different people
would be killed

raid after raid
night after night
week after week
ton upon ton of bombs

Hundreds of people
selected to live or to die
by the slight tension
of his foot
the slight tension

of his foot
caused a greater tension
in his mind

The insurance clerk
now twenty-three
suffered a breakdown
was taken off bombers
and once again
became a clerk.

When thinking about the middle years,
it is mainly the deaths you remember,
particularly if you have not had any children.
The major deaths are far and away
the biggest event of your life.

Well, Mr Briggs,
I'm afraid the
prognosis for your
wife does not look
very good.

SHAME

One December day,
Jean and I
went for a walk
on the Downs.

As we set off,
She moved so slowly
I began hopping
on one leg.

"Look, I can hop
faster than you walk.
For Heaven's sake
Come on!"

At the time,
I didn't know
she was dying.
Nor did she.

THE PROGNOSIS

In the evening,
after they told me,
I was cutting her toenails
on the hospital bed.
Cutting, thinking,
but saying nothing
about the prognosis.
Cutting, thinking:
This evening
will be the last time
I do this.

LYING IN HOSPITAL

One day,
in the ward,
she says: I wonder,
am I going to die?
Of course you're not,
I say.
We look at each other,
till I turn from the bed.
Did she see the lie?
But no more was said
in the ward,
that day.

Darling Raymond Briggs
I am trying to write
you a letter. It is not
easy to see it is all
blurred. The Visitors
are here & I am
listening to all the
Voices trying to make
sense out of it.
I hope you feeling
O.K.! Please take

care of yourself —
I love you with all my
heart for always
I do hope I will be
out of here soon, so
that I can be with you
there is a beautiful
Nurse on tonight she
came in when I screamed
over the pudding, her
eyes are beautiful & she
is black. See you
tomorrow lots of love
from Jean xx xxx

CHRISTMAS EVE we went for drinks up the road and then on to friends for a meal in Ditchling. And then the following morning, her abdomen had swollen up from chest to crutch, which frightened us to death. I felt awful getting the doctor out on Christmas Day, but he came like a shot, and got her into hospital immediately. My wife died on 21 February of leukaemia.

It happened so quickly, we had been on a late holiday in France in October, swimming in an open air pool in Dieppe, and four months later she was dead and buried. It was uncanny, the speed of it.

We didn't know she was ill apart from getting these enormous sweats and feeling terribly hot. I remember her sitting here, where I'm sitting now, and pulling her jersey off because she was so hot. I remember I said, "Goodness, it's not hot . . ." but that must have been part of it.

She was well used to hospital because she had schizophrenia, that was why we had no children. With her type of schizophrenia you are more or less ill all the time, feeling too hot, feeling too cold, or having shuddering attacks rather like epilepsy, all sorts of things were going on, so that is perhaps why the leukaemia got lost amid the general mass of her other symptoms.

I've never seen such suffering in my life, with schizophrenia and leukaemia going on at the same time, she was having terrible attacks of fear and panic, a terrific amount of shouting and screaming. She took an old shirt of mine in to hospital to hug, a lucky, comforting thing, like a child with a toy.

We had a very strong relationship, properly in love and all that, and in a sort of romantic way I did think of doing myself in, but of course you never do.

Hospital visiting seemed to occupy all my time, just trying to fit in meals for instance, the main

visiting was 6pm to 8pm, so it was too early to eat before you went, and too late to eat when you got back.

She looked perfectly good except she lost a lot of weight, but she didn't look shrivelled up, she looked quite radiant, actually. She was a rather beautiful woman. She was 43, but she looked 20 years younger, a tall, long-legged, good-looking woman, God knows what she was doing married to me . . . but anyway.

She wasn't actually told she was going to die. I think she guessed it, but we never had the nerve to discuss it. I don't know whether you should or shouldn't.

It was late at night, I was in bed, and they phoned up to say she had gone. I hardly knew what to do. I wanted to know what date it was because they rang just about bang on midnight, I asked was it Tuesday or Wednesday?

And then I went round to the hospital; she was sitting up in bed, looking absolutely normal really. They were very kind at the hospital, they said I could sleep there if I wanted, but I didn't fancy that. I sat there for a bit, I didn't stay very long. They gave me a huge brandy, literally a pintful. I said, "I can't drink all that . . ." but they let me drive home, so I don't think it was as fierce as it looked.

After a death, most people are surrounded by relations, but she had no brothers or sisters, nor did I, and my parents were both dead, they had died the year before, so they weren't here to come and hold my hand or anything. I lost my mother, father and wife in two years, that was an appalling couple of years.

The period between death and the funeral is a dreadful time to get through; the day of the funeral you can sort of heave a sigh of relief and think, right, new start, but all the time the person is unburied you are living in this no-man's land, not knowing

what to do with yourself.

I nearly went to the pictures the day before the funeral; I was wandering round Brighton trying to pass the time, but I thought, I can't go to the cinema the day before my wife's funeral. The funeral was just up the lane. It is a nice country church, and my publishers turned up from London, which was terribly kind, I didn't even know they knew. And then friends and I set off for a massive two-day walk to Eastbourne after a great meal in an Italian restaurant.

But it was a dreadful time. I wouldn't want to go through that again. I have got a diary of it all which I can never bear to look at. I read about two lines and think, oh my God, I am not going through all that again: the handwriting gets more and more upset, and then there are blank pages where I couldn't bear to write anything at all, and there is no point in sweating through that again really. So I try not to think of Jean at all.

RAYMOND BRIGGS TALKS TO DANNY DANZIGER

THE INDEPENDENT, 18 NOVEMBER, 1991

JEAN 1973

Dear God,
What a first-rate show it was!
Stars of the Double Bill,
Ladies and Gentlemen –
Schizophrenia and Leukaemia!
Backed by a Full Supporting Cast
Of Valium, Largactil and Cortisone.

Such a merry dance they had –
The very theatre shook.
Dear God,
I wish you could have been there.
You should have heard them
Screaming, screaming, screaming
Until the final curtain.

JEAN 1975

It is eleven weeks
Since I visited my wife's grave.
It is not far away,
Just up the lane.
Five minutes' walk.
She has been dead
For two years and seven months.
The grass is long and rank,
When I cut it.
The ants are swarming.
Nettles topple over the grave.
There are no flowers.
Just two empty pots
Full of dirty water.
Neither of them have I seen before.
Someone has been there.
One contains skeletons of roses,
The other pot is empty.
Someone has left a jam jar
Against the stone,
And bird lime runs down its face
To where the lettering says:
IN LOVING MEMORY

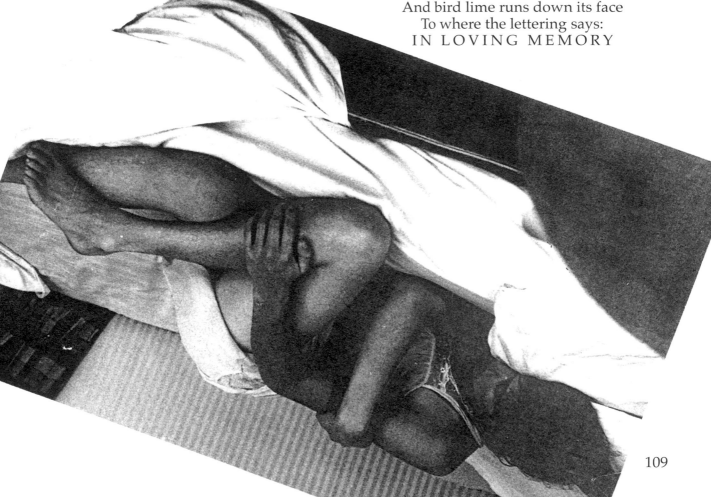

IN LOVING MEMORY
2005

This year,
For the first time,
I forgot
my wife's birthday.

Days later,
I got a pot
of primroses
to plant on her grave.

But I forgot.
Now, the primroses,
still in the pot,
are fading.

*

Coming home
from a weekend away,
I find the primroses still
on the windowsill.

I had forgotten
to water them.
The plant is alive,
but the flowers
are dead.

TWO GRAVES 1988

This year, for the first time,
I forgot the anniversary
of my wife's death.
I was not even certain
of the date.
The diary for 1973 says
21 FEBRUARY
JEAN
in big, black capitals.
The rest of the month
is a blank.

Her grave
is thick with beech leaves,
a rotting holly wreath,
still there from Christmas,
iron pots, with dead stalks
in stinking water,
primulas budding,
snowdrops in bloom.

At home, in the garden,
I notice, among the dead leaves,
a bit of fallen wood.
When I turn it over,
earwigs run out, slugs crawl.
The faded lettering,
in big, black capitals, says
KITTY 1963 – 1980
I had forgotten her as well.

I suppose you are allowed
to forget a cat.

THIRTY YEARS AGO

They say teeth last a long time.
Teeth my lips touched
thirty years ago.

Are they still there,
in the coffin darkness,
grinning in the skull?

Good teeth, firm and strong,
A smile, a loving, laughing smile,
thirty years ago.

TWO DEATHS

The dead badger
lay in the road,
just near the churchyard.
I pick up his hind paws,
still warm,
and drag him to the hedge.
Under the hedge,
he lies on ivy leaves.
My wife lies under the ivy leaves,
just inside the hedge.
The badger, dead for perhaps
thirty minutes or so,
Jean dead for thirty years,
or so.

So perhaps you should not feel guilty.
You have to go on, even if it means forgetting,
and feeling guilty when you remember.

PARTY

It's always hard to believe
in the deaths.
As the years go by,
it gets still harder.
You see them as they were,
you hear their voices,
remember their smiles.

Especially those you knew
as children,
saw them grow up,
learning to speak, learning to write,
riding their bikes.
How can they all be dead?
How can they have died so long ago?

Sometimes I imagine them
all together, in this room,
smiling, laughing, talking . . .
a kind of party.
Year by year,
the room gets more crowded,
new departures keep arriving.

Distant relations,
friends and neighbours,
people down the pub,
old acquaintance
not to be forgot.
Still they come.
So many of them!

It's getting overcrowded now.
They are all packing in.
Soon there won't be room
for me to go on living here.

NEGLECTED GARDEN

My garden is too full,
overgrown with memories.
Unpicking the tendrils
from her neck,
I draw them down
from her shoulders,
uncovering her breasts,
her waist,
her thighs.
The ivy peels away
like a clinging gown,
then lies at her feet
in the shade.
Filling the garden,
the memories still cling,
but now, they too,
are overgrown.

DEADLY NIGHTSHADE

One night,
when she is dead,
her shade
will fade with the light
of day.
She will become
a shade of the night.
Not deadly,
only decayed,
not even a flower,
just a ghost.

JOAN 2008

Joan has died.
Ninety-two years old.
Her brother dead.
Both sisters dead.
Husband long dead.
One son, sixty,
arranged the funeral.
Younger son in hospital,
on a distant continent.
In the crematorium,
a mobile phone
heard the service for him.
No friends came.
All had gone,
long ago.

Afterwards,
we few who were there
were all meeting,
greeting, drinking
and laughing,
remembering Joan,
dear Joan,
who had gone,
ninety-two years old,
not long ago.

ADDRESS BOOK

The Book of Life
is an address book.
Family and friends,
colleagues and acquaintances.
All life is there.

Clearing out a drawer,
I come across an address book,
its spine hanging off,
the yellowing pages loose
and brown at the edges.

Family and friends,
colleagues and acquaintances,
over a hundred gone.
An old address book is
The Book of the Dead.

ARTWORKER

Delivery of Fabriano 5,
My favourite paper.
SMOOTH LUCIO 160 grams,
50 by 70 centimetres,
Fifty sheets.
One hundred bits of "art".
Will I ever use it all?
Have I got one hundred ideas?
Even if I have,
Is there time?
Will I need another delivery,
or will this lot
see me out?
Fabriano 5, it says,
PAID IN FULL.
One less clause
for the will.
One more pause
for thought.

EVENING

After dinner, as usual,
the candle is burning down,
yet again.
Every evening, it burns lower,
still bright,
but its light
sinks ever deeper,
as dusk closes in.

This evening
the rabbits scurry
over the lawn,
feeding,
hurrying, hurrying.
They know little time is left.
Daylight is fading.
The darkness is coming.

FOUR BODING

Three men,
three dogs.
Almost every day
we meet on the path,
or up by the church.

Bruce with Sam,
a spotted handkerchief,
red and white,
for a collar.
Scotsman Bill with Robbie,
the water-mad dog,
long-haired and dripping wet.
Me with Jess,
our manic Border Collie.
The dogs are all friendly,
so are we.

One day,
I realise two weeks have passed.
Where are they all?
Holiday? Illness?
Death?

I phone.
Bill distraught.
Robbie dead.

Bruce away,
girl says.
Sam dead.

Last saw Sam,
on his own,
rogering a bitch,
halfway up the hill,
happily panting.

Last saw Robbie,
wagging his tail,
rolling in a puddle,
squealing with glee.

Three men,
one dog.

I am the oldest man.
Jess the youngest dog.

Two down.
Four to go.

COLD NEIGHBOURS

Just because I'm paranoid,
doesn't mean the neighbours *aren't*
turning their backs on me.
First, next door but one, on the left,
disappears without a word.
We'd never even spoken.
Can't have caused offence.

Then, next door, on the right,
old lady disappears,
widow of well-known surgeon.
Had barely had two words with her.

Then, next dor on the left,
professional knitter,
one evening, puts down her knitting,
disappears.
Never seen again.
Didn't even say goodbye.
Knew *her* very well indeed.

Then, up the road, on the other side,
two retired schoolteachers,
clever ladies, written books,
first one, then the other, disappears.
Never spoke to either of them
except on the phone.

Next door to them,
dear old Pat and his missus,
ex-Africa, Colonial types,
gin and tonics at sundown.
Knew them very well.
Went blind, poor chap,
then buggered off.
She waited around, bought a flat,
but later, disappears.

Up at the end,
on the other side,
two charming ladies,
old-fashioned, arty,
both swanned off
without so much as a toodle-oo
or see you soon
or cheerio
tat-a
pip pip.

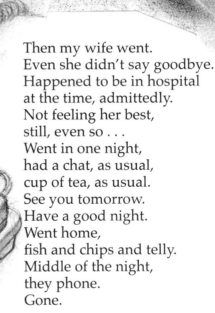

Then my wife went.
Even she didn't say goodbye.
Happened to be in hospital
at the time, admittedly.
Not feeling her best,
still, even so . . .
Went in one night,
had a chat, as usual,
cup of tea, as usual.
See you tomorrow.
Have a good night.
Went home,
fish and chips and telly.
Middle of the night,
they phone.
Gone.

Whaddya know?
Here today, gone tomorrow, eh?
Have a good night?
Seven houses, ten disappearances.
Is it me?
Can't be, can it?
Hope not.
I got a theory.
I reckon it's something to do with
time.
That's it. I'm too old.
That's why they're all
cutting me dead.

THE CANDLE

The old candle
is burning down to its end.
I sit, holding the new candle,
waiting.
It can't be long now.
The pool of wax deepens,
almost drowning the struggling flame.
Suddenly,
the wick falls, lies on its side,
still burning bright,
but smaller and trembling.
Quickly,
I light a new candle
in the dying flame,
and stand it beside the candlestick,
waiting for the last moments.
For a while,
the tiny flame flutters on,
then suddenly grows still,
gleams bright, and dies.
Quickly,
before the wax can harden,
I bury the end of the new candle
in the remains of the old.
The wax wells up,
seals it round,
grips it, holds it
firm and upright,
a tall flame steady at its tip.

Hours of life in it yet.

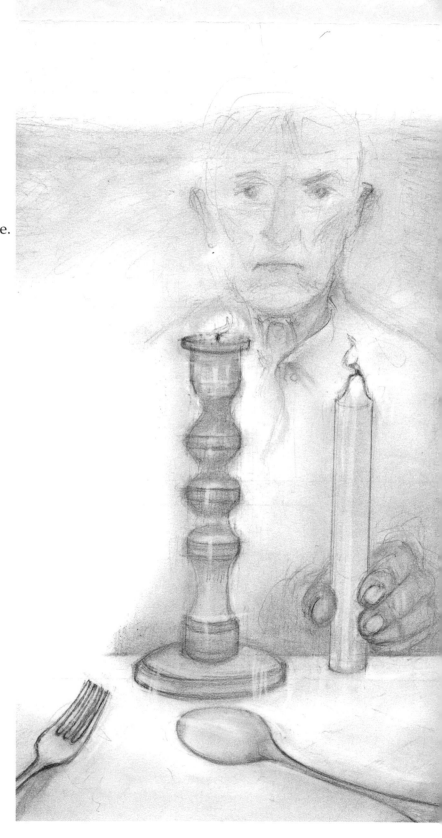

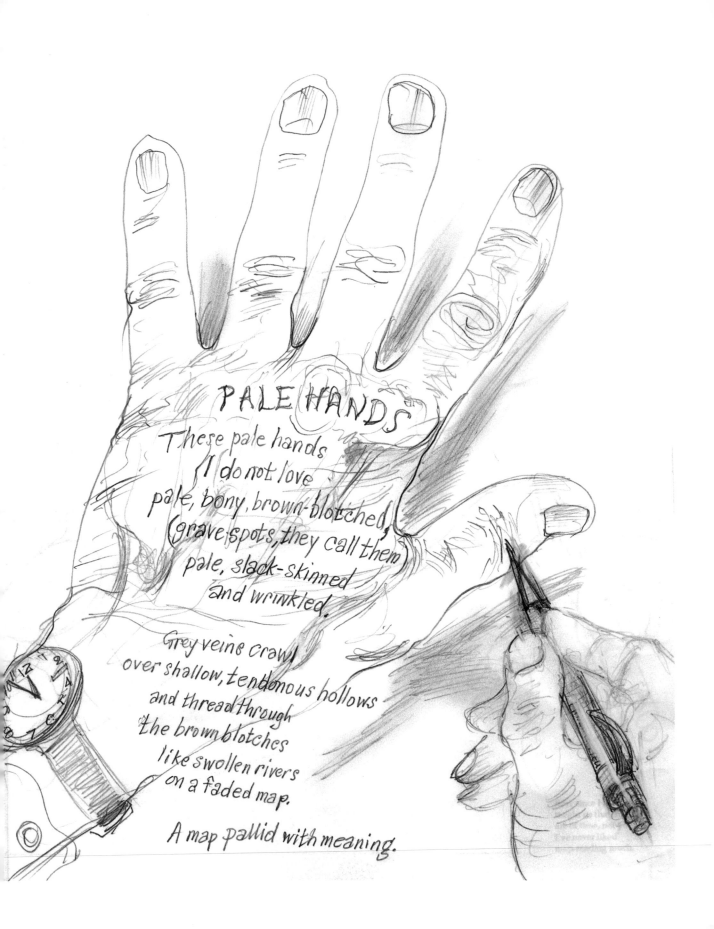

PALE HANDS

These pale hands
(I do not love
pale, bony, brown-blotched,
(grave spots, they call them)
pale, slack-skinned
and wrinkled.

Grey veins crawl
over shallow, tendonous hollows
and thread through
the brown blotches
like swollen rivers
on a faded map.

A map pallid with meaning.

NEVER TO BE FORGOTTEN PHRASES
or Intimations of Mortality

I have to warn you that after this procedure
you may become impotent, doubly incontinent,
and you may need a colostomy.

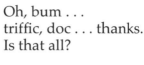

Oh, bum . . .
triffic, doc . . . thanks.
Is that all?

On the other hand, in old age,
there comes a growing indifference.

LILAC FOR LOCAL

General Election.
Went along to vote tonight,
A citizen's duty and a right.
White form for General,
Lilac for Local.
Didn't know there was a Local.
Better put a cross
Against some name.
Make them both the same?
Why not?

Flimsy plywood booth for voting.
Three-inch pencil
Tied with string.
So easy, voting.
Doesn't cost a thing.

Lib Dems are OK,
So make them both Lib Dem?
Keeps it simple.
White slip for General box.
Lilac for Local.

We take it all for granted.
Easy come, easy vote, easy go.
Even Hitler got himself elected.
Red and white for General.
Black for Local.

Black for everybody.

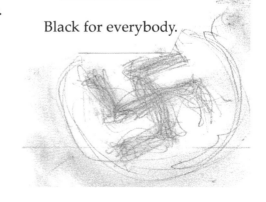

I know that last page
like the back of my hand.

PRODNOSE: Oh dear. No! No!
Spare us.

Everyone complains about the loss of respect, but some loss of respect was welcome as it was part of an unjust class system. Sadly, there is now also a loss of respect for the dead.

Also, as you get older, the world seems to be getting worse. It isn't, of course, but it feels as if it is. Every generation feels the same.

UNITED REFORMED

The path up to the church
and past the gravestones
is littered with fag ends.
From the tall stone pillars
a plastic sign is flapping
RISTORANTE PIZZERIA.

At the side of the church
rubbish bins, beer barrels,
plastic crates, a gaping fridge,
a rusting freezer cabinet,
and a heap of broken chairs.
A black hosepipe
lies across two graves,
then coils back
into a pool of liquid.
On the wall,
sprayed letters spell
CUNTS

Some of the graves are recent,
mourners are still leaving flowers.
Then, right against the hedge,
and covered in miniature cyclamen,
is a tiny grave.
        In Sweet Memory of
        a Darling Daughter
        and Grand Daughter
        Who Died
        5 March 1993
        Aged 10 months
"We'll always love you Sweetpea"

THE SKELETON

The skeleton sits by the electric fire,
in front of the television –
News, quiz games and football.
In the hall an avalanche of letters,
offering loans, holidays, life insurance.
But the skeleton isn't interested.
Christmas cards, birthday cards
and presents, all filled with good will.
Merry Christmas. Happy Birthday.
The skeleton had two extra birthdays
after she was dead,
and two extra Christmases.
The cards are there to prove it.
You could say it was unfair,
cheating Time like that.
But the skeleton doesn't care.

The phone rings, the doorbell rings,
but the skeleton sits on,
its bones warmed by the electric fire.
A newspaper lies across its knees,
crossword half filled in,
as yellow and faded
as the remnants of her skin.
Her chair stained
and half filled in,
in front of the television.

In the park, children play,
daffodils bloom, then fade.
In the flat, the electric fire burns on
through the heat of the summer.
Autumn leaves fly past the window.
Snowflakes drift down,
settle, and melt away.
The daffodils bloom again.
Still the skeleton sits by the electric fire,
in front of the television,
through the seasons,
again.

At one time, the skeleton worked in advertis-
ing.
It made phone calls,
travelled on the tube,
had love affairs,
and a family.
Now, it had missed her fortieth birthday.
But the skeleton is past caring.
It just sits by the electric fire
in front of the television –
News, quiz games and football.

Until the Housing Authority,
concerned about the rent arrears,
drills open the lock.

FOP

Rigid, unmoving, upright,
clamped inside a metal frame
like an art installation,
the statue seems almost alive.

Bright-eyed,
wearing glasses,
trousers and shirt,
it looks about fifty.

Then the eyes move.
It is alive.
A statue, not carved,
but made of bone.

A second skeleton
of its own bone,
installed slowly,
over a lifetime.

Silent, remorselessly,
year after year,
flesh made bone
by the gene ACVR1.

Neck locked,
arms seized,
ribs fused,
knees solidified.

Fibrodysplasia
Ossificans
Progressiva
FOP.

ADD AND SUBTRACT

Under ten,
every year counts.
A world of difference
between three and nine.
The add up has begun.

Over seventy,
every year counts.
A world of difference
between seventy-three
and seventy-nine.
The countdown has begun.

If, by then,
you can still count.

LIFE MATHEMATICS

At school,
I was always hopeless at Maths.
But, in the Infants' Class,
the numbers were simple.
I am five.
I am six.
I am seven.
It was called Addition.

In the paper today –
Men: Expectation of Life
Seventy-eight.
I am seventy-three,
in a few weeks' time,
seventy-four.

Here, in the top class,
having passed through
the Fourth, the Fifth, the Sixth,
we are now in
the Leavers,
sorting out our books

and belongings,
ready for the goodbye
handshake from the Head,
sitting alone in his dark study,
waiting for us to knock
on his door.

Seventy-eight,
minus seventy-four,
equals . . .
The numbers are bigger now.
It's called Subtraction.
It ought to be easy,
but I cannot understand this one.
(I prefer Addition.)

78–74 =
No, sorry sir,
I can't grasp it.
It just doesn't add up.
But then, at school,
I was always hopeless at Maths.

MARATHON HOTEL

Entering the seventies race
is like going through a door
into an unfamiliar hotel room.
It is a different space,
this ante-room,
an age away from other rooms
lived in before.
Also, the view is fairly poor.
The room next door,
the eighties, is quite near,
but the management say
you are unlikely to be allowed in there.
Its view is even poorer, by the way.
There is no room service,
nor is there a coach
to help keep you going,
just keep going on your own,
keep on going.

The end of the marathon
is very near, but no one
will be there to cheer you on.
The white tape
is fluttering in the breeze,
ready for you to burst through,
hand in your keys,
leave your luggage,
and check out.
By the door of the changing room,
no fans will linger,
just a few friends
in sober dress.
You won't have won,
but you will have won through
to the end of your stay.
There will be no medal,
but then, there is no bill to pay.

THE LONG WALK

Everyone round here does this long walk
over the Downs.
It's not exactly compulsory,
it's just something you have to do,
a communal thing.

It's a bit tough at the beginning,
steep slopes that seem to last for ever,
but once you are up here,
it's a fairly level plain.
You come across rough patches, of course,
occasional showers and even storms,
but there are great prospects ahead
and good views everywhere.
You meet so many people,
friendships are formed,
sometimes, even marriages.

There's only a few ahead of us now.
All the leaders have disappeared
into the distance.
And they are the oldest!
Most of the group are well behind us.
Of course, the youngsters
are trailing even further back,

playing around as usual,
having a good time.
No thought for the distance ahead,
let alone the hostel.
That would mean bedtime.

It is all so pleasant up here,
in the beginning,
we thought it would go on for ever,
and just like the youngsters,
we forgot about the hostel altogether.

*

Oh, we seem to be speeding up.
What's the rush?
It must be all downhill
from now on,
that's why it feels faster,
after the long, slow trudge
up those early slopes.

Oh, look, there's the hostel,
that dark building,
down in the hollow.
They haven't put the lights on yet.

It looks rather grim, don't you think?
Those cold stone walls,
that wet, slate roof.
Rather unwelcoming.
Lifeless.

No one about.
I hope they know we're coming.
Look, the door is opening.
They must be expecting us.
No need to hurry,
they said we won't be turned away.
I wish there was a light on in there.
I'm glad you're with me.
So am I. Hold my hand.
I think we have to go in alone.
You go first.
No, you.
It's not up to us,
I think they come and get you.
We don't have a choice.
We'll just get a bit nearer,
then someone will come out
and beckon us in.
They'll say "We're ready for you now."

It seems they undress you,
wash you and put you to bed.
Luxury, I suppose,
but I'd rather do it myself.

I don't like the look of it.
The light is fading.
It's almost dusk
it's so dark down here,
in this hollow,
so damp and cold.
That old couple ahead of us,
they're going in.
There. They've gone.
It must be us next.
Still no light in there.
They just went into the darkness.

Oh look, they're beckoning me.
I'd better go on ahead.
I always said I'd get there first.
Goodbye, love.

GRANDCHILDREN

A shaft of inspiring light amid
the gloom of old age.

TOUCHED

Girl 4 says:
You go to Grannie's
every day, don't you?
Yes, that's right.

She's your – *partner,*
isn't she?
Yes, that's it.

A small hand
touches inside my arm.
Boy 2 says:
You're my partner, Raymond.

I STAND CORRECTED

Crossing a big field
with the little boy,
hand in hand,
he says:
"I wonder if there are
any tiggers in here?"

"Tiggers?" I say. "Tiggers?
Oh yes! I see –
A. A. Milne."

"No!" he says, firmly.
"A. A. Malign."

LITERACY TEST

The four-year-old gave his grandmother
a screwed-up handful of paper.
Inside was another scrap of paper,
the size of a postage stamp.
On it was written:

> Read it out, Grannie!

> *Well . . . it just says . . . Miles . . .*

> No! It says QUANTITATIVE.
> THE END.

> *Oh, I see . . .*

> Do you know what "quantitative" means, Grannie?

> *No, Miles, I don't.*

> It means you can't push people over.

BEDTIME 2002

FOUR YEAR OLD: Don't pull the blind down, Grannie.
I want to see the faraway land.

*

BEDTIME 2003

GRANNIE: Shall I leave the blind up, Miles?
So that you can see the faraway land?

FIVE YEAR OLD: That's not the faraway land, Grannie!
That's the Downs.

TOY TIME

In the dusty attic,
three yellow plastic ducks.
On their wings,
a splash of green,
on their beaks,
a splash of orange.
Beside them,
a blow-up plastic boat,
its airless sail
flopping over,
its red hull limp.

The little boy
had played with them
for hours,

in the wash basin,
talking aloud to them,
telling endless stories,
adventures, battles,
and storms at sea.

Now they are abandoned,
the ducks still smiling
under the dust,
the boat empty,
almost flat.
The little boy
now plays with
space robots,
rockets and ray guns.

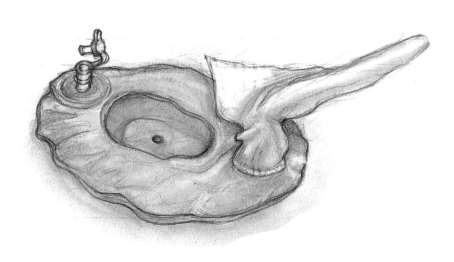

CLOCKWORK CANOE

The clockwork canoe
used to paddle round the bath,
its motor whirring,
the big penguin in his red beret
plying his yellow paddle,
propelling the canoe
in circles,
round the little boy.
The baby penguin in his red beret,
in the bow,
keeping a look out.

The waves made by
the little boy

always swamped the canoe,
sinking it to the bottom of the bath,
paddle and propeller
still whirring,
under the soap suds.

Now its motor is jammed,
its key won't turn,
but still it rests
on the rim of the bath,
waiting for its next voyage.
But the little boy
has gone.

BLUEBELL RAILWAY

We sit in a carriage
of the Bluebell Railway
with the little boy,
waiting, waiting,
for the train to start.
It is his first ride
in a real puffer train.

Waiting
waiting
waiting

Suddenly,
with a hoot
and a lurch,
the train ierks forward.

"We're impregnant!"
cries the little boy,
his face alight.

"What's that?"
I say.

"We're impregnant!"

"Oh . . .
Oh . . . yes . . . so we are."

GUDUNK GUDUNK
GUDUNK GUDUNK
GUDUNK GUDUNK

Already he is pressed to the window,
where the fields, the trees,
the sheep and the deer,
the clouds of smoke,
the puffs of steam,
drift slowly by . . .

GUDUNK GUDUNK
GUDUNK GUDUNK
GUDUNK GUDUNK

WISDOM

Five persons in car
front: us
back: three children
girl 8
girl 6
boy 4
us not talking
then out of the blue
girl 8 says
Raymond's got nibbly chocolate pants on
girl 6 says
I expect he's got a chocolate willy
boy 4 says
if he's got a chocolate willy
he could cut it off and eat it

Out of the Mouths of Babes
and Sucklings come forth
Freud and Goya.

PLAYROOM PICTURE

"What colour shall we paint the boat?"
I asked.
The three year old replied
    "Dark white."
"Grey, you mean?"
    "No!" he insisted,
    "Dark white."
Obediently, I painted the boat dark white,
and thought of painting the sea
    a red-ish green,
    the sky
    a yellow-blue,
    the sun
    a purple-ish orange,
    and the funnels of the boat
    a light black.

133

GRANDCHILDREN: DAY

Hooray! Hooray!
The children are coming
Today! Today!
They're staying the night,
And such a delight
it will be!

They'll leap on the bed
and sit on my head,
then drag all the bedding
downstairs.
They'll have piggy-backs
until my back cracks,
and competitive games
in the garden.
I won! I won!
Did not! Did not!
Did! Did! Did!
Hate you!
Pig! Pig! Pig!
Now, come on, you two,
I say.

What a day!

And so it goes on, until
the cavalry comes over the hill.
Their car! Their car!
The parents are here.
They're here!

Thank Heaven! Thank Heaven!
The children are leaving.
It's such a relief
to see them all go!
But then there descends
the quiet and peace
of an old country church,
and the silence and stillness
of snow.

An emptiness.

So we'll have a sit-down
and a doze by the fire,
and clear up the mess
in the morning.

PICTURE BOOK

Look, said Grannie,
There's a big spider
And there's his web.
There's a little spider
And there's his web.
No, Grannie! said the three year old,
That's not the little spider's
Website.

GRANDCHILDREN: NIGHT

In bed, asleep,
uncannily still,
the children lie at ease,
but strangely contorted.
The boy, as usual, half fallen out,
his head on the floor.
They seem so silent, so motionless,
hair spilled over the pillows,
their breathing soundless,
invisible,
their faces at peace.

Can these be the same children?
Are they still breathing?
Are they alive?

ANNATOMICAL ACCURACY

Having given the eight-year-old girl a little leaping
ballet dancer, supported on a wire rod
I said: It's not very nice the way
          that wire goes through her pants
          and into her bottom.
She replied: It doesn't go into her bottom,
          it goes into her vagina
          where the babies come out.

When I was eight years old, I had no idea
where babies came from and had never
heard the word "vagina". The subject was
never mentioned at home nor in five
years at secondary school. Not a word.

It seems almost unbelievable now
that there was no sex education at all.
Not one word about it at home,
nothing in primary school and most
surprising of all, not a word at secondary
school.
      This ignorance caused untold anxiety
to me and probably thousands of other children.
      My mother, born in a two-up, two-down
terraced house, with eleven children conceived
in it, was told nothing about menstruation.
She ran home, terrified, with blood running down
her leg, thinking she was dying.

A couple of years later, there came a further example
of how times had changed.
     12 year old: With this on my front,
                     I look as if I'm pregnant.
     10 year old: Well, if you are pregnant,
                     it must be Jack Simmonds.
     12 year old: I can't be pregnant,
                     I haven't started my periods yet,
                     so it must be Jesus.
It was inspiring to hear a young girl unconsciously
brushing aside centuries of sexual repression and shame,
together with religious myth, all in a single sentence.

KNITTED PEOPLE

In a corner of the playroom,
the little knitted people
sit in a row,
huddled against the wall,
waiting.

A funny old lady,
with woollen flowers in her hat.
A boy chimney sweep,
with a woollen brush in his hand,
and soot on his cheeks.
An old man with a walrus moustache
and woollen carrots in a knitted basket.
A nurse in blue with a red cross
on her woolly white chest.
A plump ballerina with fat pink legs,
in a lumpy woollen tutu.

Now the children have outgrown them,
the little people sit in their corner,
abandoned.
Once they were loved, cuddled,
taken to bed,
friends and protectors
against the dark.

Shall we give them to the charity shop?
we ask.
No! Don't!
But you never play with them.
No, but we still like them.
We want them to be there.

So the little people sit on,
in their corner, waiting.
Abandoned, but not forgotten.
They will not grow up,
Nor will they grow old.
They know, one day,
Someone will come.

SUMMER MEMORY

Something half forgotten,
lost in the heap of lawn mowings.
Sky blue.
What can it be?
Looks almost like a boat . . .
I pull it free –
it *is* a boat.
Then I remember . . .
a boat-shaped paddling pool.

The children,
laughing in the summer sun,
the little boy,
splashing in the pool, naked,
then standing up to pee
over the side,
proudly showing off
his tiny penis
to his sisters,
shrieking with laughter
and rolling around
on the lawn.

Today, they no longer need
a boat-shaped paddling pool
to be cool.

Why, children, did you reach the world so late,
Coming to me just when my years are spent?
Young things draw our feelings to them;
Old people easily give their hearts . . .

PO CHU-I, *c* 820 AD
trans Arthur Waley

BED SONG

Early one morning, the nine year old
quietly opened my bedroom door
without knocking,
crept across to the bed
and climbed in beside me.
Too old now for a cuddle,
not in the mood for a wrestle,
he said, "Do you like Python music?"
"You mean songs? Yes." I said.
He began to sing in his choirboy voice
and I joined in.
We sat side by side, in our pyjamas,
singing together:
    " Every sperm is sacred,
      Every sperm is great,
      If a sperm is wasted,
      God gets quite irate."
Etcetera.
A very good way to start the day.

Acknowledgements to
Michael Palin/Terry Jones

Death hovers around us every day.
Somehow, we close our minds to its closeness,
even when it is just outside the window
or is staring at us from the television.

SAUSAGE AND MASH

They sit in front of the telly,
Oven-ready meals on trays.
"There's not much on tonight."
    HITLER'S HOLOCAUST
"Oh, dear. Do we want that?"
"Well, there's not much else on."

Forks lift baked beans to mouths.
Fork-lift trucks tip corpses into pits.
"Nice sausages, aren't they?"
"Yes, Organic. English.
Supposed to be pure."

"Oh, it's the commercials.
Turn the sound down, will you?
I can't bear the noise."
"Nice gravy, isn't it?"
"Yes. Low salt.
Supposed to be healthy."

"Oh, it's starting again.
Dreadful, isn't it?
Poor people . . .
Those little children . . .
How could they?"

"Beyond belief, oh –
There's *Come Dancing* at nine.
Is there any left-over trifle?"

LUXURY

High in the sky,
an arc from the far horizon,
a fine thread of white.
Ahead of the thread,
a speck
six miles high.

They sit in the speck
in the stratosphere,
chattering, glancing
through the papers,
sipping coffee, champagne,
free in first class,
being massaged, manicured,
pampered.

Around them,
a hundred tons
of lethal fuel,

outside, inches away,
death.
No oxygen, no air,
sixty degrees sub-zero,
a dead zone.

Far below,
Siberian wastes
drift past,
mile after mile,
hour after hour,
treeless hills,
nameless rivers,
black lakes.
A dead land,
as remote as the moon.

Was the night yesterday?
Is it tomorrow now?

MILE AGE

Driving to my friend's house,
I notice the mileometer –
39,998.
Will it be 40,000
before I get there?

Now, don't be childish.

I drive past her house,
Down to the racecourse –
39,999.
Back to her house,
still 39,999. Curses.

Now, don't be childish.

So, past her house again,
down to the level crossing.
Halfway there –
40,000!
Hooray! I've done it!

Now, don't be childish.

40,000 miles!
I turn round and drive
back to my friend's house.
Satisfied.

Childish.

ON WE GO

She says she is sad,
And I sigh.
So, am I bad-tempered
because she is sad,
or is she sad
because I am bad-tempered?

Either way,
it's all very sad.

And it makes me bad-tempered.

Age does not make us childish,
as they say.
It only finds us true children still.
                              GOETHE

As at seven, so at seventy.
                    Jewish proverb

Throughout life you can never quite believe how old you are.

Hey mister! can you tell me the time?

Me, mister. I'm 9½.

I must look really grown up.

Yes, it was terribly Jimmy

and just then this dreadful old fog came out

She must have been THIRTY! if she was a day

Can I give you a lift home after this? I've got a SCOOTER!

No thanks. My husband is calling for me in the car.

MARRIED! HUSBAND! CAR!

AHH! She must be really OLD.

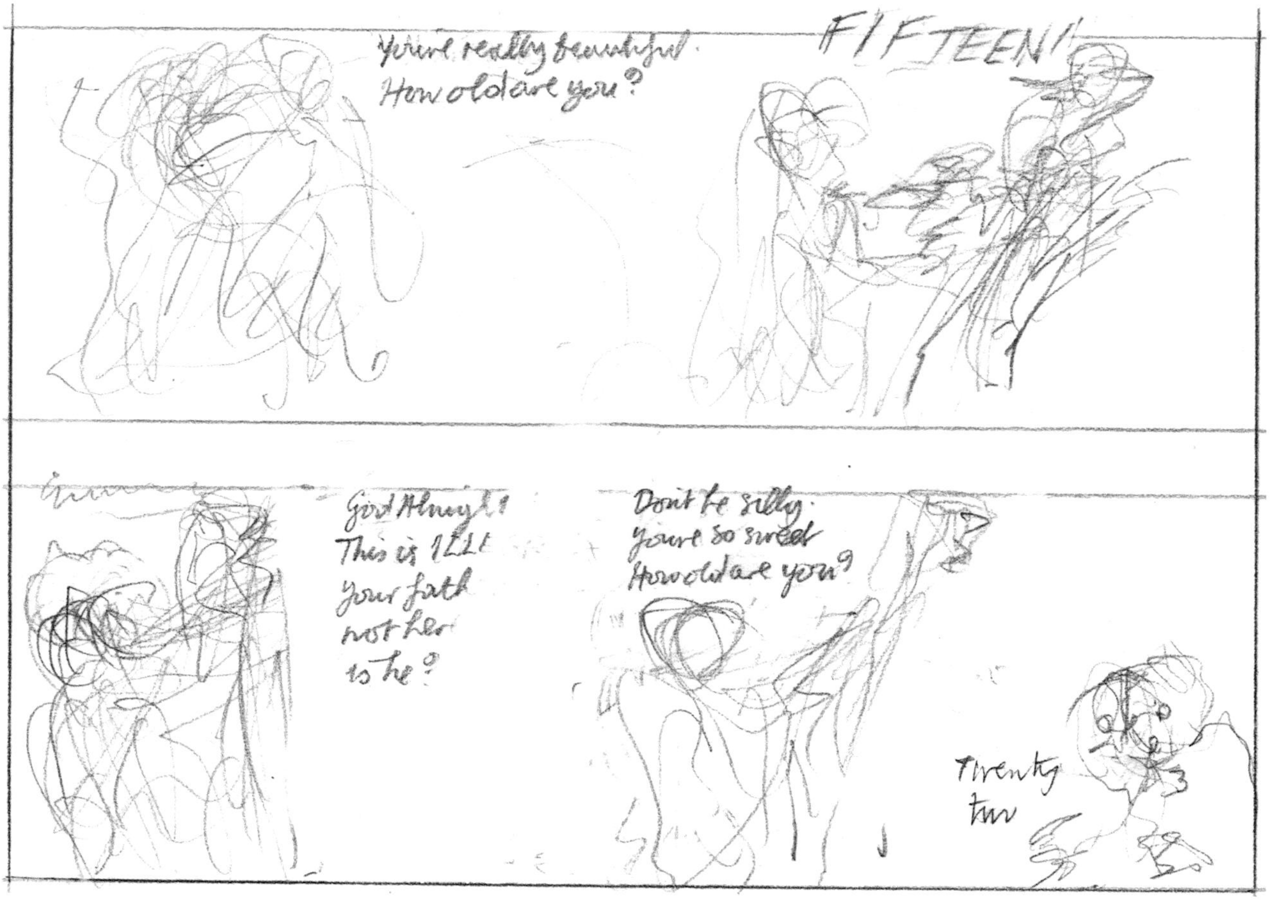
You're really beautiful
How old are you?
FIFTEEN!
God Almighty!
This is ILLE
Your fath
not her
is he?
Don't be silly.
You're so sweet
How old are you?
Twenty
two

PRODNOSE:

Oh, dear!
Here Mr. B is putting in some cartoons he scribbled down donkey's years ago.

There's nothing I can do about it, I'm afraid. You'll just have to wade through the stuff, I'm afraid; or skip it.

I should skip it if I were you. Life is too short.

PHRASES, ALLUSIONS & PROVERBS
Amended for the Elderly

AND DEATH SHALL HAVE NO DOMINION.
I would't bet on it.

A HOUSE IS NOT A HOME . . . Thank God.

ARE YOU SITTING COMFORTABLY? Not since
the operation.

EAT, DRINK AND BE MERRY,
FOR TOMORROW comes too soon.

PUT YOUR BEST FOOT FORWARD
Both of mine need attention.

MY CUP RUNNETH OVER.
Blast! Wife offering napkin.

HIT THE GROUND RUNNING.
Tripping down steps.

Not DRESSED UP AND NOWHERE TO GO.

I KNOW WHERE I'M GOING . . .
unfortunately.

ANYONE FOR TENNIS? You cannot be
serious.

ANOTHER LITTLE DRINK WON'T DO
US ANY good.

THOSE BLUE REMEMBERED HILLS . . .
Really? We did? When?

GO, MAN, GO! We can't afford *more*
drycleaning!

IN THE COUNTRY OF THE BLIND,
THE ONE-EYED MAN can't find his glasses.

AND SO TO BED, but only to sleep.

IF AT FIRST YOU DON'T SUCCEED, throw the packet away.

I'M JUST GOING OUTSIDE.
Well, don't lock yourself out this time.

THE SOFT UNDERBELLY.
Bathroom mirror.

I SPY STRANGERS!
Oh, lovely! It's the grandchildren.

I KNOW WHERE I'M GOING.
They brought you back twice yesterday.

THE SKULL BENEATH THE SKIN.
Shaving mirror.

OUR DAY WILL COME gazing out the window at passing hearse.

THE PASSWORD
to peace in old age

The Joy of NO

Just say NO
NO dressing
NO driving
NO parking
NO queuing
NO waiting
NO train
NO tube
NO crowds
NO noise
NO chattering
NO speeches
NO taxi
NO waiting
NO train
NO driving

Home
meal
wine
sofa
missus
telly
paper
book
dog
bed
read

peace

RULES FOR THE ELDERS

REMEMBER YOU DO NOT HAVE TO DO ANYTHING
YOU DO NOT WANT TO DO
NO ONE EXCEPT THE LAW CAN MAKE YOU DO ANYTHING

GUARD YOURSELF
DO NOT FEEL OBLIGED
DO NOT FEEL GUILTY
DO NOT CARE ABOUT BEING WELL THOUGHT OF
YOU ARE ENTITLED TO BE YOURSELF

DO NOT LISTEN TO PERSUADERS AND FLATTERERS
THESE PEOPLE ARE OFTEN SEEKING THEIR OWN ENDS
AND ARE USING YOU FOR THEIR OWN PURPOSES

ABOVE ALL DO WHAT YOU WANT TO DO
AND SPEAK YOUR MIND CLEARLY AND FIRMLY
IN THE BEGINNING
WHEN ASKED TO DO SOMETHING YOU DO NOT WANT TO DO
SAY NO STRAIGHT AWAY
DO NOT PREVARICATE

FOLLOW YOUR INSTINCTS
DO WHAT IS RIGHT FOR THE INNER YOU
NOT WHAT YOU THINK IS CORRECT FOR THE OUTER YOU
OR FOR THE NEEDS OF OTHERS

YOU HAVE BUT LITTLE TIME LEFT
EVERY DAY IS PRECIOUS
DO NOT WASTE A DAY
ABOVE ALL DO NOT LET OTHERS WASTE IT FOR YOU

Inscribed on a tomb in Westmeston churchyard, Sussex: 1534

This book of yours –
where's the plot?
Where's the conflict?
It lacks narrative drive.

'Course it does, dumbo!
ND is bollocks.
Leave ND to the
buggering novelists.

They only bung it in
because they
can't draw.

This is much more subtle –
an in-depth, psychological
musing upon the themes
of old age and death . . .

and nostalgia
for the past.

Sounds pretentious
tripe to me.

Yes . . . well,
        maybe . . .
for once you may
have a point.

SOON

THE VIEW

The trees are growing,
the view is going.
The distance draws nearer,
year on year.
Soon the horizon will be gone.
Distance will be
just across from here,
no distance at all.
A dark hedge
will block the view,
and shut out the light.

LOST

The driver turns and says,
Which is it, sir?

Which is it?

Which house?

House?

Your house, sir.

My house?

Where you live.
I've got to drop you off.
They didn't tell me the number,
just the road.
I've got the road.
We're there.
Could you point it out, please sir?
Where you live.

Where I live?

VISITING FLORENCE
IN THE HOME

Visiting Florence in the home,
I look across at another lady,
Straight-backed, dignified, stately.

She seems to be looking my way,
so I almost respond,
But her face is vacant.

Her gaze looks neither at me nor past me.
Her colourless eyes are glassy,
Not sightless, but seeing nothing.

Later, when her visitors gather,
A woman's voice cries out
"I'm your daughter."

HOME VISIT

Visiting her mother in the home,
daughter and mother
sit together at a table.
I don't like this table,
says the mother.
Your mother always sits here.

IN THE HOME

The man who sits beside her,
Every day, holding her hand,
Believes she is his wife,
Whose name he cannot remember.

Her husband,
Who does not remember,
Every day, visits her.
He thinks she believes
The man who sits beside her,
Every day, holding her hand,
Is her husband.

But she thinks
The man who sits beside her,
Every day, holding her hand,
Is her lover of long ago.
His name, she can remember.

THE KEY

The old man
lives alone with his wife.
He doesn't wander about outdoors.
He wanders about indoors,
windows closed and locked,
doors closed and locked.

He likes to be locked in.
He fears being locked out.
Day and night,
he wears his front door key
on a string around his neck.
His key to peace of mind.

He falls asleep, holding the key,
and dreams of being locked out.
His wife, kept awake
by his nightmare,
lies in her bed,
longing to open a window.

When she does fall asleep,
she dreams of running, running
over the hills,
under the moon,
her arms spread wide,
her hair blowing free.

THE SHEET

The old man has wet his bed.
His wife takes the sheet off the bed.
When the daughter calls,
The sheet is on the floor.

Mum, why is the sheet on the floor?
    He wetted the bed.
Why don't you put it in the machine?
    Oh . . .

The daughter puts the sheet in the machine.
Mum, when it's done, switch it off.
Put the sheet in the dryer, OK?
    Oh . . .

When the daughter returns, the machine is off.
Mum, why is the machine off?
    It was making a noise.
Mum, you know it makes a noise.
    Oh . . .

The daughter switches the machine on.
When she returns, the sheet is on the floor.
Mum, why didn't you put it in the dryer?
    Oh . . .

The daughter puts the sheet in the dryer.
Mum, when it's done,
Switch it off and take it out, OK?
    Oh . . .

NO MORE THANK YOU

Lately, the old man
had been eating very little.
Today, when his daughter
came to take his tray away,
he had eaten almost nothing.
The old man said
he didn't want any more.

When his daughter
asked the old man
if he wanted the television,
whilst she saw to his nails,
he said there was nothing on.
Then he closed his eyes
and said nothing,
whilst she saw to his nails.

The old man said
he didn't want the doctor,
but when the doctor came,
the doctor said to the old man:
"This could be dementia."
Even then, the old man
just closed his eyes
and said nothing.

When the doctor had gone,
the old man said
he didn't want the television,
and didn't want anything to eat.
Later, when his daughter
came to take his tray away,
he had eaten nothing.
The old man said
he didn't want any more.

THE NAVY BOYS

"We'll be all right now,
the Navy boys are here!
The dying woman
gave a cheerful grin,
grasped the safety rails
around the hospital bed,
and nods towards
hospital porters
pushing trolleys.

She loved the Navy,
the Empire, India,
and her Naval grandson,
Commander Dane.

Smiling happily,
she gripped the iron rails
all around her.
"This is the Dane stronghold!
We'll be all right now,
the Navy boys are here!"

MORNING TEA

When the daughter calls,
her mother says:
"Your father's still in bed.
He's having a lie-in."

The daughter looks down
at her father's face,
then leans over him,
listening . . .

Her mother says:
"He had such a peaceful night,
I didn't want to wake him."

The daughter touches her father's hand:
    "Daddy?"
The hand is cold as stone.
The mother says;
"I'll get him his tea."

The daughter stands,
Straight and still,
eyes closed, lips trembling,
while her mother sets out cups
in the kitchen.

Her mother calls:
"Tell him he's come to the end
of his ginger biscuits."

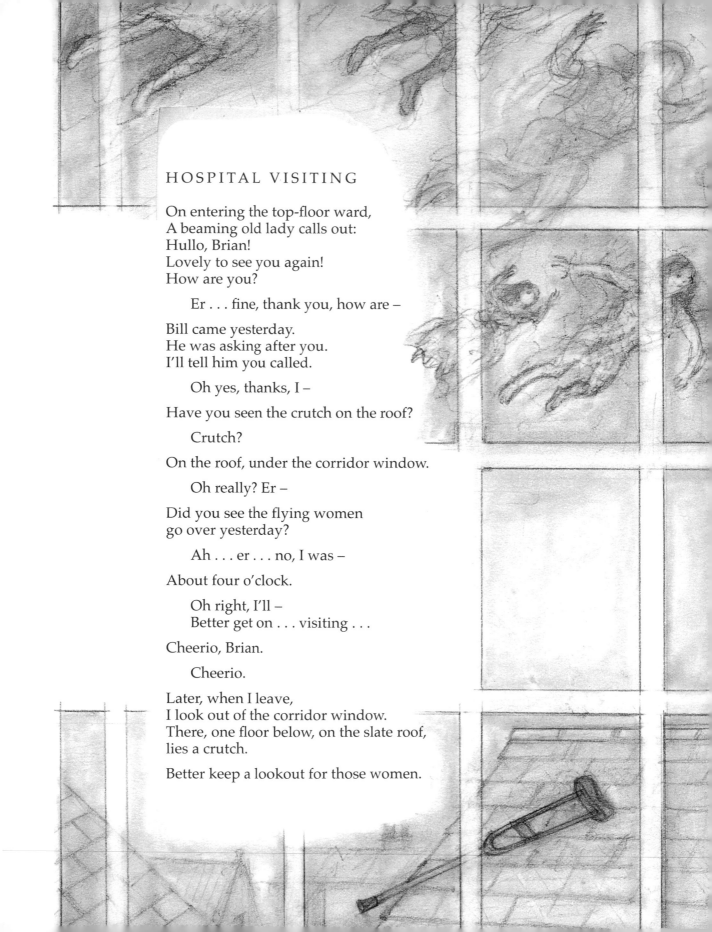

HOSPITAL VISITING

On entering the top-floor ward,
A beaming old lady calls out:
Hullo, Brian!
Lovely to see you again!
How are you?

Er . . . fine, thank you, how are –

Bill came yesterday.
He was asking after you.
I'll tell him you called.

Oh yes, thanks, I –

Have you seen the crutch on the roof?

Crutch?

On the roof, under the corridor window.

Oh really? Er –

Did you see the flying women
go over yesterday?

Ah . . . er . . . no, I was –

About four o'clock.

Oh right, I'll –
Better get on . . . visiting . . .

Cheerio, Brian.

Cheerio.

Later, when I leave,
I look out of the corridor window.
There, one floor below, on the slate roof,
lies a crutch.

Better keep a lookout for those women.

LIFE TIME IDIOMS

First the time of day
no time like the present
then always pressed for time

tick tock

Always keeping time
and working against time
to be all in good time

tick tock

Must lose no time
biding your time
for the time being

tick tock

Then passing the time of day
time after time
times without number

tick tock

By making good time
having a good time
time flies

tick tock

the time of your life

tick tock

But time will tell
and not before time
in less than no time

tick tock

part time
time on your hands
killing time

tick tock

Then before your time
time out of mind
time's up

tick tock

time was
tick
half a tick

tick off
no time at all
time off

IDIOM

A group of words
established by usage
as having a meaning
not deducible from
those of the individual
words.
OED p. 908

T.A.T.T.

Tired All The Time?

asks the Doc,

wearily.

He's tired all the time,

too.

tick tock

tick doc

Life, time's fool,
And time, that takes survey of all the
world,
must have a stop.

SHAKESPEARE
Henry IV, Part I

TIME WILL TELL

They say
"At this moment in time,
there is a waiting list
for the home.
There is no vacancy
at present,
but a place may become available
soon.
Maybe in three months' time,
after the winter.
Maybe tomorrow.
No one can say,
it all depends . . ."

They will let us know
in good time.

AM I WORRIED?

Alive and well,

they say.

Alive, yes,

but well?

Only time will tell.

*

Yes, I am.

GOING IN

Returning a book,
I knock at a neighbour's door.
After a lifetime,
the eighty-eight year old
opens the door.

Her face, pale and gaunt,
the skin almost transparent,
her faded eyes, magnified.
She clutches the door
in arthritic grip.

As I offer the book,
she laughs.
Oh no! Not another one.
She raises her hands in mock horror.
Thank you, she says.

I'm going in tomorrow.
It's a nice place,
but my books . . . oh, my books!
There's no room in there.
No room at all.

Again she laughs.
All my things!
A lifetime of things!
Thank you, goodbye.
Come up and see me sometime.

Still laughing,
she closes the door,
tomorrow,
for the last time,
on a lifetime.

WHAT'S THE DATE?

Every year,
we live through the date
of our birth,
Our Birth Day,
so, we celebrate.

Every year,
we live through the date
of our death,
unaware.
Nothing to celebrate there.

Is it today?
Was it yesterday?
Will it be tomorrow?
No one can know.
No one can say.

SELF DOUBT

They say that
in old age
you lose touch
with old friends.

But maybe,
in old age
it is old friends
who lose touch
with you?

BIRTHDAY

On his grandson's birthday,
the old man always phoned.
Never missed.
This year, no call came.
When they phoned, no answer.
Anxious,
they drove to his house.
He was sitting alone,
in an upright chair.
Urine on the cushions,
diarrhoea in the kitchen,
vomit in the garage.
His diary had stopped on Tuesday.
This was Saturday.
He was still alive,
just.
Unable to move or speak.
The ambulance came
and took him away.
One went to the hospital.
One cleared up the mess.
The children wandered about.
The old man died on Sunday.
He never spoke.
After all,
There was nothing much to be said.

THE MAGIC OF DISTANCE

Please mind the gap
between the platform and the train.

And please mind the gap
between the aged mind
and the modern world.

They tell me the train doors
at our village station
are opened by satellite.

When you begin to think
that the world has gone mad,
you know that you've been on it too long.
It's time to get off.

A friend in Folkestone,
booking a hire-car for Italy,
talks to someone in Oklahoma.
"Sure thing, M'am.
Have a nice day, M'am."

Our grandchildren
play backgammon
with anonymous strangers,
in unknown countries.

Phoning about train times in Hove,
I talk to someone in Calcutta.
"Wod dime train
are you be gedding, sir?"

Decades ago,
didn't Laurie Lee say
the magic of distance
was being destroyed?
Fortunately for him,
he's far away now,
safely in the distance.

Perhaps we will only re-discover
the magic of distance,
when we cross over the line
to the down side
and travel on
to the terminus.
We should feel some distance there.

Please mind the gap
between the platform and the train.

This must be my stop,
coming up at last.
It is quite a distance
between the platform and train,
but at least
I won't have to open the door.

JOURNEY INTO SPACE

Yesterday,
heart thumps.
Uneven pulse –
bump . . . bumpbump –
space
bump . . . bump . . .
10 . . . 9 . . . 8 . . .
bumpbumpbump
space
Is this IT?
Or just
the beginning of IT?
The launch pad.

Today,
faint chest pains,
on the left.
That's where the heart is,
isn't it?
On the left?
bump . . . bump . . . bump –
space
7 . . . 6 . . . 5 . . .
bump
bump – space . . . bump –

Space
is when it stops,
isn't it?
4 . . . 3 . . . 2 –

Space

INDUSTRIAL DISPUTE

I always say
I have to keep reminding myself
I am over seventy.
But that's just the mind
reminding itself.
The mind believes itself
to be younger.
It looks down on the body.
After all, it is the head,
up above.

But, down below,
the body needs no reminding.
It knows it is over seventy.
It can prove it.
There is evidence.
It lets the owner know,
night and day.
But the owner
pretends not to notice.

Occasionally, the body goes on strike.
Up above, the owner
is forced to change his mind,
if only for the duration of the strike.
But then the owner ignores this reminder.
He doesn't listen to the body,
screaming quietly inside.
Eventually, when it stops screaming,
there will be a down-tools,
a walk-out, a shut-down.
That's when the owner
will sit up and take notice.

But he won't sit up,
because, by then,
he'll be lying down.

CRAYONS

Grey,
White,
Flesh,
and Black.

Once again,
as always,
the coloured crayons
have been tidily sorted
into their jars.

Reds, Crimsons and Pinks,
Yellows, Ochres and Oranges,
Cerulean Blues and Ultramarines,
Emerald Greens and Viridians,
Sienna Browns and Umber Browns.

Grey,
White,
Flesh,
and Black.

"You've got enough there
to last a lifetime."

grey white flesh

and black

no need to order more

crayons

WAITING

One day, when I am dead,
This house will be waiting –
The flannel stiffening by the bath,
The soap cracking.
        The bed not made.

In here, the desk, a pen,
Crayons and pencils pointing,
The chair facing the view.
The telephone ringing
        now and again.

Pictures of Dad with his milk crate,
Mum an Edwardian maid, posing,
Eighteen, but seeming like twelve,
Their wedding photograph fading,
        Ash in the grate.

The Guinness lamp from when the pub sold up.
Aunt Mag's woollen patchwork covering
The junk shop sofa.
Last week's paper, yellowing.
        Milk on the step.

All these silly things
Will be waiting
For the Executor to walk in,
With smart suit and shoes shining.
        To tidy up.

FUTURE GHOSTS

Looking round this house,
what will they say,
the future ghosts?

There must have been
some barmy old bloke here,
long-haired, artsy-fartsy type,
did pictures for kiddy books
or some such tripe.

You should have seen the stuff
he stuck up in that attic!
Snowman this and snowman that,
tons and tons of tat.

Three skips it took,
and a whopping bonfire out the back.
Thank God it's gone,
and he's gone, too.
He must have been a nutter
through and through.

HOME

No choice
but to enter
sometimes kept
waiting in turn
to be allowed
to enter

to be allowed
no choice
of what to eat
or when to eat it
no choice but to
wait in turn
for the bathroom
wait in turn
for the lavatory

just like school
just like the army
but this time
there is no
waiting in turn
to be allowed to go
home

this time it means
waiting in turn
to be taken
to where
you will be kept
waiting in turn
to enter

When I left home before, after more than twenty years in my parents' house, it was not painful as it meant FREEDOM! INDEPENDENCE! GIRLS! Onward and upward!

This leaving will be the exact opposite: *loss* of freedom, *loss* of independence. No girls. Backwards and downwards.

Instead of breaking free of the childhood world, this will be like entering a childhood world again.

Larkin called it "The whole hideous inverted childhood".

Better have a last look around . . .

I can't believe this is happening.

All my pictures!

Jean's paintings and her self-portrait drawing.
Pip, Squeak and Wilfred original by A. B. Payne,
after I wrote asking for a drawing
when I was about thirteen.

"Moon", too, the great cartoonist
of the *Sunday Dispatch*.
DRAWN WITH THE GREATEST
OF PLEASURE FOR MASTER R. BRIGGS.

A Charles Keene original –
one shilling and sixpence in 1960.
In a box on the pavement outside the shop,
being sold for the frame.

Self-portraits by students
I worked with . . .

Four originals by Steve Bell,
a Snowman by Fritz Wegner
and two original cartoons by Trog,
one of the Snowman
and one about *When the Wind Blows*.

The blanket Auntie Mag knitted,
been on the sofa for years.

The coal scuttle we had at home
for over forty years, and has been in use here
for over thirty years.

The cushion Jean made
in the mental hospital.

That Windsor chair.
Dear old Uncle Joe died in it,
in the back garden in Sydenham.

The other Windsor chair
I bought in a Boy Scout jumble sale
for one and ninepence,
in 1956.

The notorious crotch log,
picked up beside the road,
just as a log to burn on the fire.
Got home, turned it over and saw what
it was.

The slate shove ha'penny board
and the Guinness lamp,
from when the Half Moon sold up.

Mum and Dad's
dining-room clock.
When it chimes, it's like
being home again in the 1940s.

Mum outside her house in Sydenham,
when she was about seven or eight,
Over a hundred years ago . . .

Will there be room for ANY
of these in this poxy place?

All ready, sir?   Been in the   Forty years!
                   house long, sir?   Expect you'll miss it
           Yes.   quite a bit then,
                             Over forty after all that time.
                             years.   Bound to.

                                                  Still, never mind, eh?
                                                  Life goes on.
                                                  Can't stop progress,
                                                  can we, sir?

Time marches   Gone tomorrow . . .
on, as they say. Yes.   Like singing
Here today and   let's hope so   Gone tomorrow . . .   do you, sir?
gone tomorrow . . .   " ♫ Tomorrow is
       etcetera   A lovely day . . . ♫ "   Well . . .

                             Not interested,   Tomorrow a gentleman's
                             sir?   coming in to show us
We've got   Yes,   his stamp collection –
a sing-song   I'm sure.   a Mr Morrison.   Terrific.
tonight, sir,   I'll see.
as it happens.   Thanks.

Very jolly.
                                              Ah! you're interested, sir?

                                                   I'll see how I feel.
                                                   I'm still settling in.

Quite understand, sir.   Next week a lady
You settle in.   is coming in to give us a talk
Take your time.   about quilts.

                                                   Quilts!

          Time . . . yes . . . time . . .
                                              Yes, sir.   Christ!
All you want, sir.
All the time in the world.   No, sir,
                                                        quilts.

172

Here we are, sir.
Plenty of room –

Chest of drawers . . .

nice big wardrobe . . .

bedside cabinet
with drawer –
oops! Sorry –
knob's come off.

Soon fix that.

Nice little radio.

Phone's down
the passage,
next to the toilet.

We can always
pop you home again, sir.
Pick up any bits and bobs
you require.

bits and bobs . . .
yes . . .
home . . .

Will you be selling
the car, sir?

I'm not allowed
to drive any more.

Friend of mine
would be interested if –

My son-in-law
will see to it.

Sorry.
It was meant to be a joke.
Is her name really Mrs Tombs?

Don't forget
the sing-song
tonight, sir.

Everyone joins in.
Doesn't matter
if you can't sing.

Mrs Tombs has done
you some nice new
curtains, sir.

What's that sir?

Very good of her,
thanks.

The final curtains.

Its curtains
for me.

Yes, sir.
Curtains for you.

It'll be the death of me.

Yes, sir.

Sir?

Funny the association
between laughter and death . . .
Don't you think?

Oh, blimey
Another joke.
This place is going to be
A laugh a minute.

"He was so funny, he knocked 'em dead."
"It was killingly funny."
"Laugh? I nearly died."
Odd, isn't it?

Er . . .
Shall I get you
a cup of tea, sir?

Don't be too long.
I may have passed over
to the Other Side.

I'll get the tea, sir.

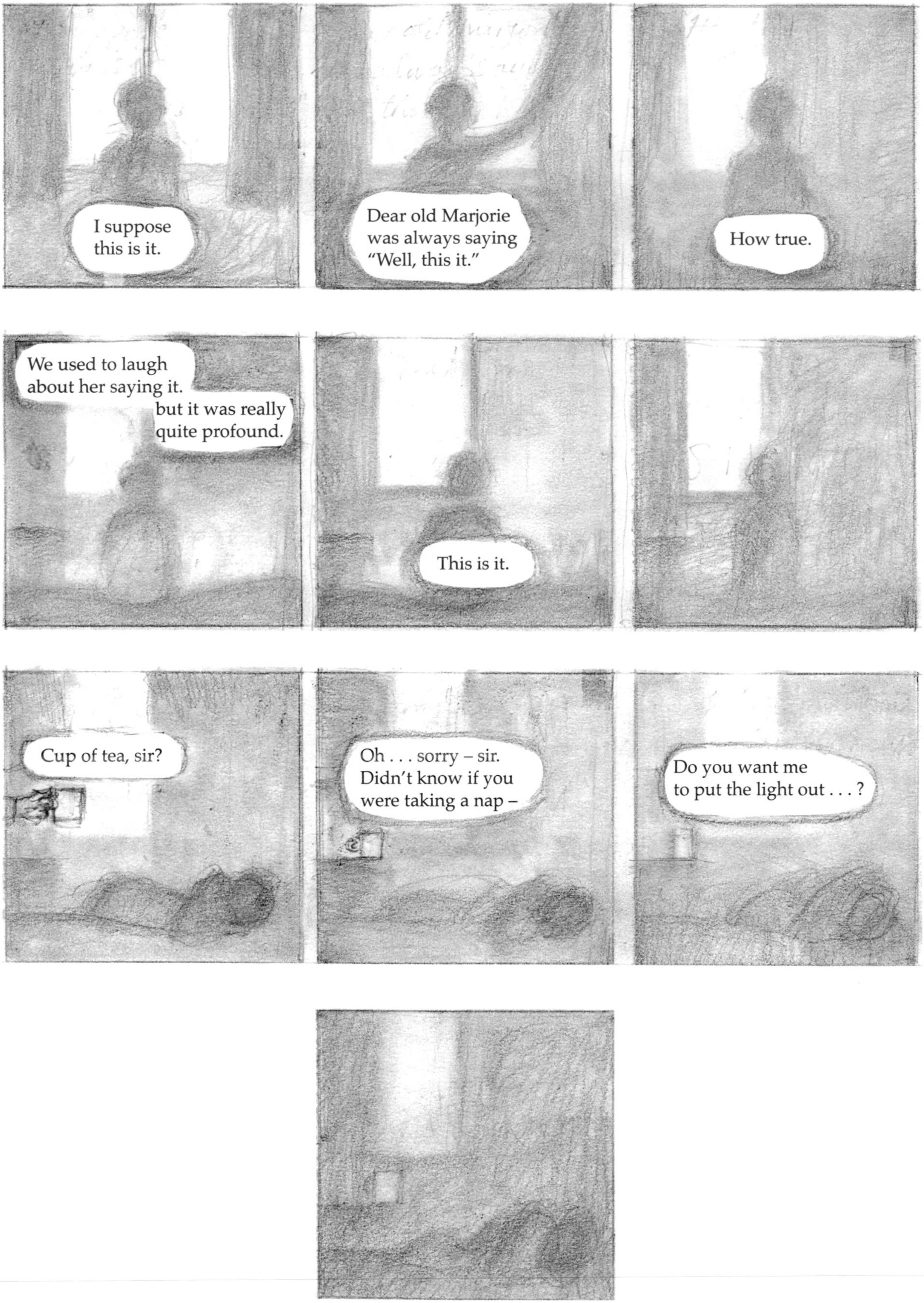
I suppose this is it.
Dear old Marjorie was always saying "Well, this it."
How true.
We used to laugh about her saying it.
but it was really quite profound.
This is it.
Cup of tea, sir?
Oh . . . sorry – sir. Didn't know if you were taking a nap –
Do you want me to put the light out . . . ?

THE END

Life is a jest;
and all things show it.
I thought so once;
but now I know it.

JOHN GAY

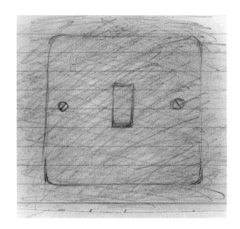

The thing to remember
is that each time of life
has its appropriate rewards,
whereas when you're dead
it's hard to find the light switch.

WOODY ALLEN The Early Essays

GRAVE

Eyeless
the skull stares
and grins
noseless
in the stench
of coffin darkness
earless
listening to nothingness
the skull
brainless
thoughtless
throat
voiceless
in the meaningless
emptiness
and silence

Well, that passed the time.

PRODNOSE: It would have passed anyway.

And I looked,
and behold a pale horse:
and his name that sat
on him was Death.

The Revelation of St. John the Divine.4
Ox. Dic. Quot (old hard back) 518b

WHAT DID I DO WITH IT?

The Age Old Problem
(or Old Age Problem) of
WHERE *ARE* THINGS?

Where is my pen?
Where is the book
I am writing this in?

I can't finish this
till I find it.

So I will have to
give up

now